Exploring with GPS

Bruce Grubbs

Bright Angel Press
Flagstaff, Arizona

Contents

Acknowledgments

Thank you to everyone who made this book possible, including Roy Rukila and Peter Levine who both did a great job of copy editing, and Duart Martin who got me into GPS with that wonderful birthday present of a Magellan GPS receiver back in the GPS "Dark Ages."

GPS Satellite

Introduction

The purpose of this book is to present a practical approach to using GPS in the outdoors. In this book, I'll show you how to navigate with your GPS in conjunction with digital (computer-based) maps and traditional navigation tools such as printed maps. The book uses realistic scenarios as well as plenty of screen shots and photos to show you how to find your way in the backcountry quickly and easily.

Exploring with GPS is also available as an ebook on the Amazon Kindle. You can view the maps, screenshots, and photos in color in the Kindle ebook on the Kindle Fire Tablet as well as on any of Amazon's free Kindle reading apps, including Kindle for PC, Mac, iPod Touch, Blackberry, iPhone, Windows Phone, iPad, and Android devices.

Although the emphasis is on self-propelled sports such as hiking, fishing, mountain biking, hunting, paddling, cross-country skiing, and snowshoeing, the information in this book is also useful for motorized activities such as back road driving and power boating.

The Global Positioning System, officially called NavStar but just called "GPS" by most people, consists of a sophisticated array of orbiting satellites and ground control stations operated by the U.S. Department of Defense and made available to all users without fees. Anyone, anywhere on Earth, can find their position within a few feet using an inexpensive hand-held GPS receiver. That simple ability has completely revolutionized land, sea, air, and space navigation as well as surveying, engineering, geographic information systems, astronomy, and many other fields that benefit from precise position and time measurements.

For outdoor recreation, the revolution continues. Not only can you find your way through the wilderness with unerring precision regardless of weather, location, or time of day, you can work with digital maps and satellite images to plan your outdoor adventures from home. You can record your trip in the field, download it to a computer, attach labels, graphics, elevation profiles, comments and photos, and then share it with friends or publish it for all to see on the Internet. As a result there is a rapidly growing amount of free trip and backcountry information on the Web.

This is not a book on technical GPS uses such as surveying, geographical information systems, aeronautical, and other specialized and professional uses of GPS. There are plenty of technical GPS books and Web sites on these subjects. If you are interested in the new activity of "E-Hiking", (trip recording with GPS and trip sharing via the Web and smart phone apps), you may want to refer to my book, Backpacker Magazine's Using a GPS: Digital Trip Planning, Recording, and Sharing.

Those who want to learn more about using GPS with paper maps, coordinate plotters, and hand held compasses should refer to my earlier GPS book, Basic Essentials Using GPS, also published by The Globe Pequot Press.

In order to keep things as simple as possible, this book is organized from basic to advanced GPS. After you master the basics, you can move on to more complex GPS techniques as desired.

You'll need a mapping GPS receiver to make best use of the techniques in this book. Refer to the GPS Receivers section in the What to Buy chapter for details on what to look for in a unit, and to this book's companion Web site, www.ExploringGPS.com, for the specific GPS receivers I currently recommend. The Web site also features a glossary which explains GPS features and terminology, and there are links to the GPS manufacturers as well as sites with more information on GPS.

I happen to own several Garmin and DeLorme GPS receivers at the moment. I like the units I have, but this is not an endorsement of any particular GPS manufacturer. It does mean that most of the screen shots and instructions in the book refer to those units. After testing trail GPS receivers with touchscreens, I find I strongly prefer units with physical buttons, so my descriptions will refer to buttons. If you have a touchscreen receiver, screen icons perform the same functions. In most cases, the same instructions apply to receivers made by DeLorme, Lowrance, Magellan, Tom Tom, and Trimble. All mapping GPS units have the same basic capabilities, but the buttons and menus will be somewhat different. You'll need to refer to your owners manual for specific instructions.

I have used National Geographic Topo! extensively, so the examples and screen shots use this product. Again, that's not to endorse National Geographic products over others. There are many other options and more are appearing all the time. Refer to the section Maps and Satellite Imagery in the What to Buy chapter for a survey of current products and free software.

Some of the GPS receiver screen shots were taken with the unit in simulator mode, which means the numbers on the GPS screens don't always match up to the current scenario. This is why some of the screen shots show unlikely speeds- walking at 10 mph and sea kayaking at 60 mph!

Remember that backcountry navigation using GPS as well as traditional map and compass tools is a serious business. A mistake, such as entering the wrong map datum or erroneous coordinates on your GPS receiver, can cost you time and energy and can even be fatal. For that reason, don't be in a hurry to buy the latest model GPS receiver or switch to a device such as a smartphone that is not primarily intended for navigation. Like all computer-driven devices, GPS receivers can have buggy firmware that can make the unit annoying and inconvenient to use or even cause it to fail entirely. I strongly recommend that you buy a dedicated trail GPS receiver that has been on the market for a year or more, which allows time for the manufacturer to discover and correct firmware defects.

And finally, while using GPS and digital maps is a blast, never forget that all this high-tech gadgetry should be used to make your outdoor experience safer and more enjoyable and is not an end in itself. It's all too easy to spend more time fiddling with your GPS and computer than enjoying the outdoors. Don't let that happen to you!

First Things First

In an age when we own an increasing array of electronic gadgets, how many of us still have something like an old VCR around the house with a time display blinking "12:00" because no one knows how to set the time on the unit? That's not because we're getting dumber, it's because most of us don't have the time to learn how to use features we don't need. It's the same thing with GPS. Even the cheapest civilian receivers have many features we will probably never use in the outdoors. That said, there are three basic GPS skills you must have to use a GPS receiver for backcountry navigation:

    1. Finding Your Position

    2. Marking Your Position

    3. Recording Your Track

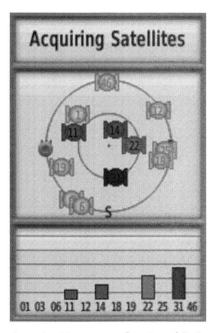

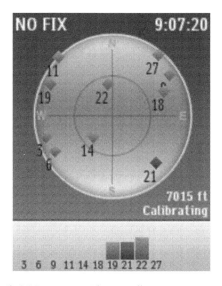

Status/position page on Garmin and DeLorme trail GPS receivers without satellite reception. The status line at the top shows that satellites are still being acquired and the receiver does not have a position fix and cannot be used for navigation.

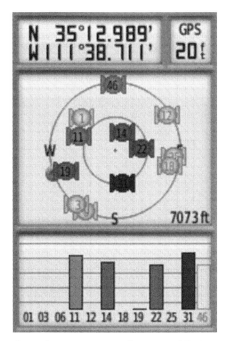
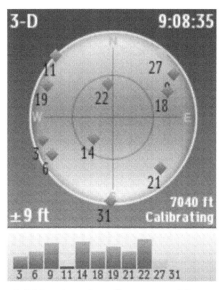

Status/position page on Garmin and DeLorme trail GPS units with satellite reception. The screen shows the GPS accuracy and the signal strength of the satellites. The Garmin receiver on the left is locked onto at least four satellites, the minimum for an accurate fix. The DeLorme receiver on the right is locked onto eight satellites.

The Where Am I? page on a Garmin nuvi shows your present location, nearest address, nearest intersection, and lets you find the nearest emergency services and fuel.

Finding Your Position

For your GPS receiver to work, it must receive very weak radio signals from satellites that are more than 12,000 miles away. This means the receiver must have a clear view of the sky, which usually requires being outside. Most GPS receivers have a status page or indicator to show if it is receiving enough satellite signals to navigate.

Turn the GPS on and watch the satellite status page or indicator. The receiver should acquire satellites within a few seconds to a minute, depending on how recently the receiver was used. Acquiring satellites is also called "locking on" or getting a "position fix." On trail GPS receivers, the satellite status page shows the position of the satellites in the sky and signal strength bars that   show how many satellites are locked on. This page also usually shows the GPS accuracy in feet or meters. You need at least four satellites for a reliable fix. On some receivers this is referred to as a "3D" fix. If the display shows only a "2D" fix, the receiver is locked to only three satellites and should not be used for navigation.

Locking on to more than four satellites increases the accuracy and reliability of the GPS fix, especially when you're moving or in a narrow canyon or other location with a restricted sky view. Most current GPS receivers can lock on to twelve or more satellites.

On most street GPS receivers, signal strength bars or an icon show that the receiver has a fix, but there's no direct indication of how many satellites the unit is using. In general, if a street GPS will accept a navigation destination, it's safe to assume that it has satellite reception adequate for street navigation.

If the receiver does not acquire at least four satellites within a couple of minutes, move to a location with a better view of the sky and stand still until the unit acquires the satellites. This may be necessary in forests or among tall buildings. In some locations, such as narrow "slot" canyons or under a metal roof, the receiver may not be able to see enough sky to acquire satellites.

Once the receiver has acquired the satellites, most trail units show your position in coordinates on the satellite status page. On some units, you may have to change to another page to see your location coordinates. On a few units you have to mark your position to see the coordinates. On Garmin street GPS receivers, go to the "Where Am I?" page from Tools to see your position coordinates. The default coordinate system displayed on most trail GPS units is latitude and longitude (lat/long), which you can change in the Setup menu. You can also see your position on the map page of both trail and GPS receivers.

That's really what GPS is all about- finding your position extremely accurately under nearly any conditions. As you move, the GPS receiver updates your position. Using this information, it can keep track of where you've been, show you how to get to a distant location, calculate how long it will take to get there, and compute your speed. After the trip, you can download the information saved in the GPS to your computer and display it on digital maps and satellite photos.

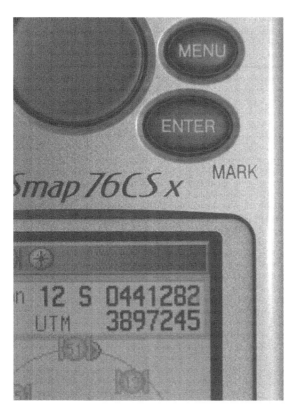

Press and hold the MARK button on this Garmin trail GPS to record your current position as a waypoint

Marking Your Position

Next, you need to know how to save your current location as a stored "waypoint". A waypoint is a geographic location described in coordinates. This is a critical GPS skill because it will enable you to find your way back to a trailhead or that spot along a road where you left your vehicle to go hunting in the forest. It will also let you mark a favorite fishing spot on a lake or record where you just placed a new geocache. You'd be surprised how many people don't know how to do this with their GPS units. A pilot friend of mine flunked his flight test to qualify as a U.S. Forest Service fire spotter because he didn't know how to mark the position of a fire with the GPS installed in the airplane.

For any backcountry traveler, being able to find your way back is a critical skill. I learned that from my hunting and fishing parents at an early age. Traditional methods, such as noting trail signs as you pass them, keeping track of your position on a map, and looking back to see how key landmarks will look on the return, are still important but GPS adds a new level of assurance. With GPS, you can mark your starting point or vehicle location with an accuracy of 30 feet or better. Of course, you can always read the position or status page on your GPS and then write down the coordinates or mark them on a map, but if you save your location as a waypoint in the GPS unit, the receiver is instantly ready to navigate back to your starting point or any other location that you've saved.

To save your position as a waypoint on a trail GPS receiver with buttons, press the "Mark" button. On a touch screen GPS unit, touch the "Mark Waypoint" icon, which is usually in the main menu.

The mark waypoint page displays a default waypoint name- usually a number. It also gives you the option to rename your waypoint and enter a comment. In the field, it's easiest to note the assigned name of the waypoint, and not bother to change it. By pressing the "ENTER" button, or the equivalent touch screen icon, you'll save the waypoint with the default name. Now you can head out to your favorite fishing spot, knowing that you can find your way back to your starting point.

To save your current location using a Garmin nuvi street GPS, from the 3D map view, tap the current location icon on the screen to go to the "Where Am I?" screen. Then tap "Save" to save your current location as a "Favorite", the street GPS term for a waypoint. You'll have the option of naming the favorite- if you don't, it will be named "Coordinates" and displayed with the latitude and longitude.

Track page on a Garmin trail GPS

Track setup page on a Delorme trail GPS

Recording Your Track

Except on the water, it's rarely possible to travel directly to your destination. Trails are built to follow the easiest terrain and experienced outdoors people do the same on a cross-country hunt or hike. If you use your GPS to navigate directly back to your saved starting waypoint, you will not follow the same route back. Traveling cross-country, you may encounter cliffs, canyons, swamps, or other annoying obstacles. That's why it's important to know how to record and follow a track on your GPS receiver.

Most trail GPS receivers can record your track (the actual route you're traveling) by automatically saving a series of waypoints as you proceed. (Street GPS receivers record tracks but you don't have as much control over the track logging function.) When you decide to return to your car or starting point, you can activate a backtrack feature and follow your exact route back to your starting point.

Before leaving your starting point, switch to the tracks page on your GPS and make certain the unit is set to automatically record a track log. This is the default on most receivers. This page gives you other options, such as to setup, save, and clear the track log. Go ahead and clear the track log so the receiver will record a new log for this trip. Under setup, check that your GPS is set to wrap when full. This means the receiver will continue to record a track log if its memory fills up by discarding the oldest track points. Since most receivers have plenty of memory, the discarded track points will usually be from a previous trip. You also want to make sure the record method is set to "Auto" and the interval is set to "Normal" or the equivalent.

In order for your GPS receiver to record a track log, it has to see enough of the sky to maintain a position fix. All but the cheapest GPS units have high-sensitivity receivers that can stay locked on in forests and other places with a partial view of the sky. This means you'll need to carry your GPS in a place where it can see as much of the sky as possible. There are several ways to do this. I've carried GPS receivers in a fanny pack or in a pocket at the top of my pack. When walking, though, it's better to have the GPS where you can use it without taking off your pack. I now carry my GPS in an after market case attached to my hip belt. That makes it easy to reach and allows the unit a good enough view of the sky to stay locked on to the satellites much of the time. Cyclists can mount the GPS on a handlebar mount. Boaters can use a waterproof instrument or deck bag. You should use a waterproof bag even if your unit is waterproof, especially in salt water.

Having set up the track log to record automatically, you can set off on your backcountry adventure knowing that you can easily and accurately retrace your route if the need arises.

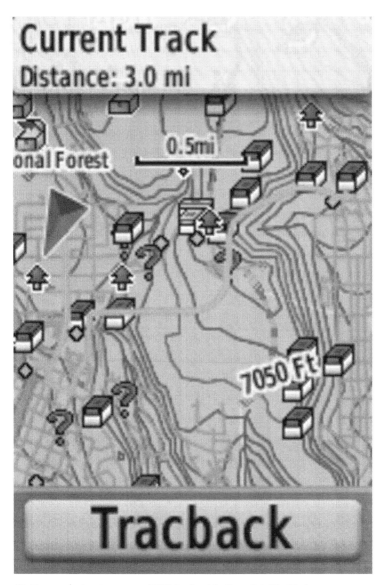

Getting ready to retrace your GPS track with Garmin's TracBack

Getting Back

Left, the find page on this Garmin trail GPS lets you find waypoints of several different types and navigate to them. Right, a list of waypoints on a Garmin trail GPS

Going Directly to Your Starting Waypoint

If you've been hunting in forested terrain with few landmarks, you'll probably want to return directly to your camp or vehicle without retracing your route. To do this on a Garmin trail GPS, press the "FIND" button, choose "Waypoints" from the menu, and choose the waypoint you created at your starting point. Then select "Go To". The receiver will switch to the map page and start navigating to the chosen waypoint.

Whether you are navigating directly to your starting waypoint, or following your recorded track back, the GPS unit creates a "route". A GPS route is just a line connecting two or more waypoints that you can follow using your GPS. If you choose to return directly to your starting waypoint, the GPS receiver creates an internal waypoint at your current position, and then creates a direct route from there to your starting waypoint. If you decide to backtrack your saved track, the GPS creates a route with many waypoints pulled from the track log. In either case, you navigate back to your starting point using the map and compass pages on the GPS.

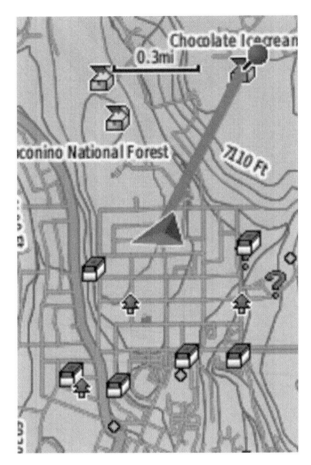

Map page showing a direct route to waypoint "Chocolate Icecream". The small triangle marks your position and also points in your direction of travel.

Using the Map Page

On most GPS receivers, your position is shown with a small pointer in the center of the map. When you're moving, the pointer also shows your direction of travel (your "heading"). The GPS doesn't know your direction of travel when you're not moving, because it needs two or more position fixes to determine your heading. To return to your starting waypoint, look at the GPS map. Notice the bold line between your position and the waypoint. That is the route you need to follow to travel directly to the waypoint. On the map, north is up, so note the approximate bearing to the waypoint and start moving in that direction. After a few seconds the position triangle will rotate to show your heading. Now all you have to do is adjust your direction of travel so the position triangle points along the route on the map and keep going until you reach your starting waypoint.

The compass page on a Garmin trail GPS showing your heading under the lubber line, the thin black line at the top of the compass dial. The bearing pointer points to the waypoint that you are navigating to.

Using the Compass Page

All GPS receivers have a compass page which shows you the direction you are actually traveling- your "heading", and the direction you need to go- the "bearing", to reach the next waypoint. The compass page on most GPS receivers uses a bearing pointer, an arrow in the compass ring that shows the bearing to the waypoint you're navigating to. Once you start moving, the compass dial rotates to show your heading under the lubber line at the top of the compass. To travel to your starting waypoint with the compass, start moving in the direction shown by the bearing pointer. Adjust your direction of travel until the bearing pointer aligns with the lubber line.

Some GPS receivers have an internal magnetic compass which works like a hand-held compass and shows directions when you're not moving. The magnetic compass must be calibrated before use.

Avoiding Obstacles

If you encounter an obstacle such as a patch of dense brush, detour around it as needed. After you're clear of the obstacle, the position pointer on the map page shows you how far you are off the direct course to your starting waypoint. As before, adjust your direction of travel until the position pointer shows that you're once again headed directly to the starting waypoint. The position pointer also shows where you are in relation to the direct route.

The compass page always shows the direct bearing to the starting waypoint, so adjust your direction of travel until the bearing pointer once again aligns with the lubber line.

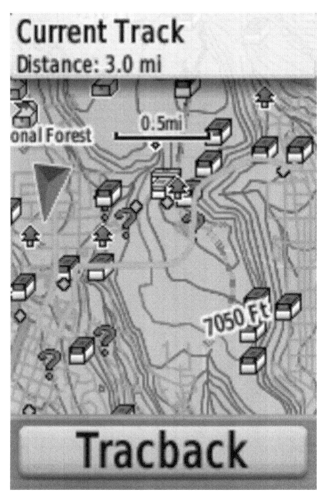

Preparing to backtrack your track on a Garmin trail GPS. The track is the solid line that starts at the position marker.

Backtracking to Your Starting Point

If you need to retrace the exact route you took to get to your present position, such as along a trail, go to the backtrack page on your GPS. On Garmin GPS units, this feature is called "TracBack". On DeLorme units, it's called "Following" a track, while on Magellan receivers, it's a "Backtrack Route". Some units let you choose the point along your track you wish to navigate to. The track may not start at your starting point if you had a previous track in your receiver before the current trip. You can zoom in on the map to make it easier to find your starting point on the track. If you saved a waypoint at your starting point, it will be shown on the map along your track. In any case, after you activate track navigation, you can navigate using the map and compass pages just as you did along a direct route.

Map page on a Garmin trail GPS while navigating with
TracBack. The TracBack route is the solid line.

Using the Map Page

Again, the position marker shows your location on the map and your direction of travel. Adjust your direction of travel so that you follow the track along the map. You can zoom in and out on the map as needed to see detail or the big picture.

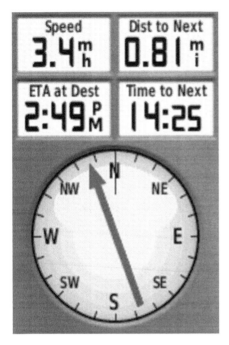

Compass page on a Garmin trail GPS while navigating with TracBack

Using the Compass Page

As you travel, the compass bearing pointer shows the bearing you should travel to follow the backtrack track. All you need to do is keep the bearing pointer aligned with the lubber line to retrace your track. Remember that the compass only shows your heading correctly when you are moving, unless your GPS receiver has an internal magnetic compass that you've correctly calibrated.

Time, Speed, and Distance

It's useful to know how long it will take to get to the next waypoint and your destination, how fast you're going, and how far it is to the next waypoint. This information is available on the compass page of most GPS receivers. Some GPS receivers put this information on different pages, but the compass pages on most GPS receivers can be customized to show the desired information.

Plan Ahead

Although this book is primarily about backcountry GPS, street GPS receivers, such as the Garmin nuvi or Tom Tom series, can be useful for finding your way to a trailhead, boat launch, or other starting point. And they're certainly useful for navigating cities and highways on the way to your wilderness adventure. Road bicyclists and motorcyclists also find street GPS useful.

Setting up a Road Trip with a Street GPS

Street GPS units come with detailed street-level mapping and points-of-interest (POI) databases built-in. This lets you navigate directly to a city, intersection, street address, or a POI. The POI database typically contains thousands of entries, so you can select your destination by spelling its name or browsing through categories such as food, fuel, transit, lodging, shopping, banks, and many more. You can also search for a type of POI near your present location, along your route, near your destination, or near a city that you specify. You have the option of saving the destination as a "favorite", which is the same as a waypoint on a trail GPS.

Where To? page on a Garmin nuvi showing icons for the types of places you can navigate to, including addresses, points of interest, and street intersections

A major difference between trail and street GPS receivers is that the maps on street GPS units are "routable". This means that the GPS receiver can plan routes to follow streets, roads, and highways. In contrast, the basemaps and topographic maps on most trail GPS receivers are not routable, meaning the GPS receiver can only create routes between waypoints or along tracks. (As you'll see in the next chapters, you can easily create routes on your computer and use the Internet to download routes created by others, and then upload them to your trail GPS for use in the field.) The routable map feature is what makes street GPS units so useful for road navigation- as long as the road you want to follow is on the GPS receiver's map.

Startup page on a Garmin nuvi, showing the satellite indicator on the upper left. The green bars show that the receiver has a position fix. The battery charge indicator is at upper right.

Before you can navigate, the street GPS has to lock on to the satellites, as described in the last chapter. If you are planning your route at home, the receiver may or may not lock on, depending on the type of roof you have and other obstacles. You don't need a position fix to plan your driving route, but if you want the GPS to lock on, go outside to a location with a good view of the sky.

Driving to Arizona's Phoenix Sky Harbor International Airport

In the first example, we assume that your wilderness adventure starts with a drive to the nearest major airport. We'll select the airport and plan the route at home before mounting the receiver in the car. Street GPS receivers have internal rechargeable batteries that last several hours so you can use them outside your vehicle.

🔍	**Page Municipal Airport** 238 S 10th Ave	118ᵀⁱ	↘
↑	**Falcon Field Municipal Ai...** 4800 E Falcon Dr	121ᵀⁱ	↙
↓	**Glendale Municipal Airport** 6801 N Glen Harbor Blvd	122ᵀⁱ	↖
↩	**Sky Harbor International...** 3800 E Sky Harbor Blvd	124ᵀⁱ	↖

Selecting the destination, Sky Harbor International Airport, on a Garmin nuvi

To find the airport, select "Where To?" from the startup page, then "Points of Interest". Next, choose "Transit", then "Air Transportation". The receiver presents a list of airports, sorted by their distance from your present location. Scroll down until you see "Sky Harbor International- T4 Departures" and select it. The next page shows the details for the airport, as well as route information. Select "Go!" to start navigating. The GPS calculates the quickest route via road, then switches to the 3D navigation page.

Sky Harbor International-T4 Departures N

3800 E Sky Harbor Blvd
Phoenix, AZ 85034

⭐⭐⭐⭐⭐   Go!

Transit: Air Transportation	
Mode: 🚗	Dist: 150.8 mi
Time: 2 hr 24 min	Fuel: $19.49

Touch Go! to start navigating on the Garmin nuvi

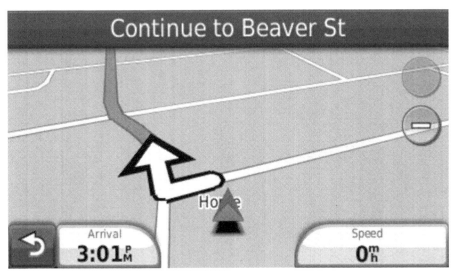

The 3D navigation page on the Garmin nuvi

As you drive, the unit graphically shows your route, intersecting streets, and gives turn-by-turn directions on screen and verbally. The 3D navigation page is especially helpful where there are numerous side roads and streets, because you can see them on the screen before you can spot the actual intersection ahead.

Some street GPS units also show traffic information, which alerts you ahead of time so you can avoid construction and accident sites. The GPS receiver can automatically calculate the best detour.

Entering a via point on a Garmin nuvi

As it happens, you have all the time in the world before your flight, so you decide to take a slower, scenic route. To do this, you need to insert a "via" point, which is the street GPS term for an intermediate waypoint. From the 3D navigation page, select "Menu", then "Where To?". Scroll down, then select "Cities". Scroll down the cities list until you see "Payson", and select it. Alternatively, you can spell the POI name. The GPS asks you if this will be a new destination, or a via point- select "Via". The GPS unit recalculates your route using the new via point. To see the route, touch the nuvi screen to switch to map view, then zoom out with the "-" icon and pan the map by touching and dragging. If the route isn't what you want, you can add more via points.

Navigating to a Trailhead

Trailheads and back roads are not always shown on street GPS units. For example, within Arizona's vast Navajo Indian Reservation, a Garmin nuvi shows paved highways and graded dirt roads but very few of the thousands of unmaintained dirt roads. On public lands, where the nuvi shows most U.S. Forest Service and county roads, trailheads and campgrounds are not shown. However, if you know the location of your destination and if the access roads are shown, you can still navigate to it with a street GPS. For example, on a Garmin nuvi, there are two ways to select a destination that is not in the POI database.

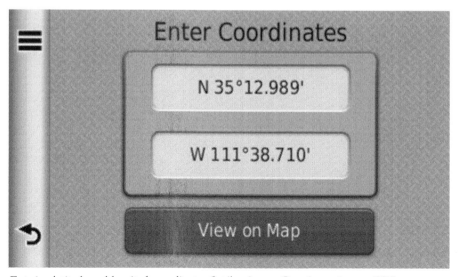

Entering latitude and longitude coordinates (lat/long) on a Garmin nuvi street GPS

The first method is to enter latitude and longitude coordinates (lat/long) directly. You can obtain these coordinates from a paper map or a guidebook that has GPS coordinates. The catch is that the guidebook may use a different coordinate system, such as Universal Transverse Mercator (UTM). There are Web sites such as http://gis.dep.wv.gov/convert/llutm_conus.php that can do the conversion or you can use a mapping program such as DeLorme Topo North America. To enter lat/long coordinates on a Garmin nuvi, select "Where To?" from the startup page, and then scroll down and select "Coordinates". After entering the lat/long, select "Next", and then "Save". Type a name for the favorite and then select "Go" to start navigation.

In this case, we're going to navigate from our home in a small town to the Kendrick Mountain Trailhead on the Kaibab National Forest, which is not shown on the GPS. We'll use the Kaibab National Forest paper map, which shows forest road numbers, and the map view on a Garmin nuvi to find the trailhead.

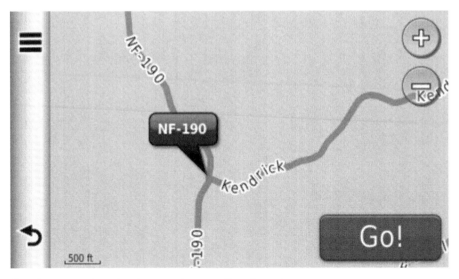

Creating a waypoint using the map view on a Garmin nuvi

To use the map view method, select "Map" on the startup page. Then touch the 3D navigation page to switch to map view. Zoom out as needed using the + and - zoom icons in the upper right corner, then touch and drag the map until you are in the area of the trailhead. Zoom in as needed to see local roads. Put the map pointer on a road to see the road number or name. When the map pointer is on the correct spot, select "Save" to give the favorite a name, then select "Go" to navigate to it. Navigation is the same as on highways and streets.

If you can't locate your backcountry destination on your street GPS, you can still use it to navigate to the highway turnoff.

Planning a Trip Using Digital Maps

One of the great things you can do with your GPS is to plan a trip ahead of time at home on your computer, download the data to your GPS receiver, and then use that data to navigate in the field. There are an ever-increasing number of digital mapping products on the market that seamlessly use topographic maps, aerial photographs, and satellite imagery to show terrain, lakes, streams and rivers, trails, roads and other features. The following examples use National Geographic Topo! (Topo! for short) because it's the program I use most. For a survey of other programs, see Maps and Satellite Imagery.

To plan a trip on Topo! and most computer mapping tools, you create a GPS route by placing waypoints on the map at your starting point and at intermediate points along the way. Before you can do this, you'll need to set up the program for your preferences. See Setting Up National Geographic Topo! for the settings used in the examples in this book.

Finding a Trailhead with Trail GPS

As mentioned earlier, many trailheads are not shown on street GPS units, nor are they in the POI database. In this case, it's often easier to use a trail GPS to plan a route to your desired trailhead or backcountry starting point. You don't have to have detailed topo maps on your GPS receiver to do this, but they do make it easier to find your way, even with a preplanned route. This example shows how to find the Sheep Trail, a very remote trailhead on the north rim of the Little Colorado River Gorge, on the Navajo Indian Reservation in Arizona. Attempting to navigate to this trailhead on my street GPS results in a route that directs you to drive across the 1000-foot-deep canyon from the highway on the south rim- without a bridge!

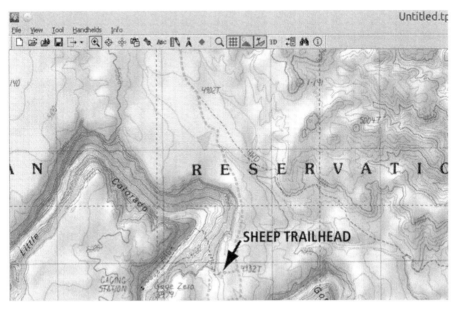

Map on Topo! showing the Sheep Trail trailhead at the end of forty miles of dirt roads. TOPO!,
©2010 National Geographic

Locating the Trailhead

You'll need to find the trailhead on a paper or digital map in order to plan the route along back roads. In this case, you can get the trailhead location from a guidebook. After reading through the guidebook description of the approach road, we can create a route in Topo! that we can follow on a trail GPS receiver.

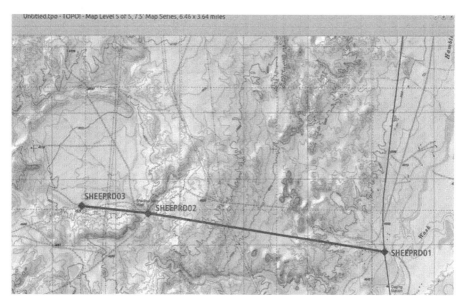

Creating a new route in Topo!. The first three waypoints have been placed and Topo! has created a route between them, shown as a solid red line. TOPO!, ©2010 National Geographic

Creating a New Route in Topo!

We're going to start the route at the turnoff from the highway, U.S. 89. In Topo!, zoom in to this location. Next, choose "HandHelds | New GPS Route" from the menu. The cursor changes to a cross, the GPS waypoint tool. Click on the turnoff. A waypoint appears on the map and the Waypoint Editor pops up. If it doesn't, right click on the waypoint you just created and choose "Properties". This brings up the Waypoint Editor. Now check the box at the bottom that says "Show this editor each time a new waypoint is created."

Now we need to give the waypoint a meaningful name rather than accepting the default. Topo! automatically names each waypoint in sequence starting with 001. You can accept the default names, but it's better to rename the waypoints to something meaningful. The Waypoint Editor lets you name the waypoint anything you like, as long as it fits the restrictions of your GPS unit. You can also add a comment. In this case, since the waypoints will be at nameless intersections, we'll start each waypoint with SHEEPRD and then add a two digit sequential number starting with 01. So the first waypoint is SHEEPRD01.

Moving Waypoints

Sometimes Topo! won't let you create a waypoint exactly where you want when Street Overlays is turned on, because Topo! pops up the name of a feature when you point to it with the mouse. You can turn Street Overlays off, using "View | Street Overlays" or you can switch off the pop-up labels. Alternatively, create the waypoint off to the side a bit and then left-click and drag the waypoint to the exact place you want.

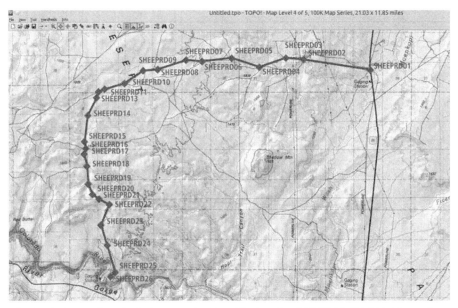

The finished route from the highway to the Sheep Trail trailhead. TOPO!, ©2010 National Geographic

Pan the Topo! map to the right to find the first road intersection. Even if you won't turn at an intersection, create a waypoint anyway. You'll see why in the next chapter, when we drive this route. Name this waypoint SHEEPRD02. When you create the second waypoint, a red line appears between the two waypoints. This is the active route that we're creating. Continue along the access road to the trailhead, creating new waypoints at each intersection and naming them in sequence. When you finish, you have a route with 26 waypoints, from SHEEPRD01 at the highway, to SHEEPRD26 at the Sheep Trail trailhead.

Editing routes and waypoints in Topo! You can edit waypoints by right-clicking on the waypoint icon on the map, or by right-clicking on the waypoint in the waypoint list at the bottom of the screen. In either case select "Properties" from the pop-up menu, which opens the Waypoint Editor. TOPO!, ©2010 National Geographic

Editing Routes and Waypoints

After you finish creating the route, you can view a list of your routes by selecting "View | GPS Waypoint List" from the menu. The pane on the lower left has a list of your routes. By default, Topo! creates a route name from the first and last waypoints. You should rename the route to something more descriptive by right-clicking on it. In this case, use SHEEPRD. You can also rename waypoints by right-clicking on them in the waypoint list. After you're happy with your waypoints and route, select "File | Save" from the menu to save the GPS route and waypoints as a TPO file.

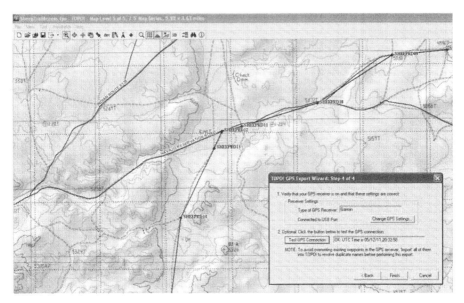

Exporting the route and waypoints to the GPS receiver with TOPO!, ©2010 National Geographic

Exporting the Route and Waypoints to Your GPS

Turn your GPS receiver on and connect it to your computer with a USB cable. Some GPS receivers require that you install a software driver before the computer will recognize it. In Topo!, click on the route to make sure it's active (it turns red when active and blue when inactive), then select "Hand Helds | Export to GPS Wizard" from the menu. When the wizard appears, select "To a GPS receiver that is now connected to the PC", and click "Next". On the next dialog box, select "Only the Active Route (displayed in red)" and click "Next". On the third page of the wizard, select the "WGS84" datum. The last page gives you a chance to check your GPS connection and change GPS settings if they're wrong. When finished, click "Finish". The active route and its waypoints will be exported to the GPS receiver. Now you're ready to navigate the route in the field, as described in the next chapter.

Sheep Trail trailhead in Google Earth. The label is in the middle of the parking loop, and a bit of the trail can be seen switchbacking into the gorge to the left of the V-shaped shadow. Google Earth, ©2010 Google

Planning with Google Earth

Satellite images are often useful when planning a trip because you can look at features that are not shown on maps. For example, in Google Earth you can see the back roads used to reach the Sheep Trail trailhead, as well as the trail itself. If you're having difficulty locating the trailhead on the topo map, you can get the coordinates from Google Earth and then create a waypoint in Topo!. Likewise, you can trace the access roads on Google Earth to find intersections and roads that are not shown on the map.

Google Earth can also be used to plan GPS routes and transfer them to your GPS, a process that requires several steps:

1. In Google Earth, use "Add | Path" from the menu to create a route line. It is best to click on each point where you need a waypoint rather than drawing freehand. Freehand routes generate too many GPS waypoints.

2. Name the route.

3. In the Places sidebar, right-click on the path, select "Save As", and save the file as a KML file (not KMZ).

4. Use a program such as GPS Babel (www.gpsbabel.org) to convert the KML file to GPX.

5. Import or open the GPX file in your favorite mapping program on your computer.

6. Create a GPS route from the waypoints.

7. Export the GPS route to your GPS receiver.

Taking a Hike

Using Topo! again, we're going to plan a hike in Arizona's White Mountains. We'll hike over the top of Mount Baldy, Arizona's second highest mountain, using the West Baldy, East Baldy, and Connector Trails.

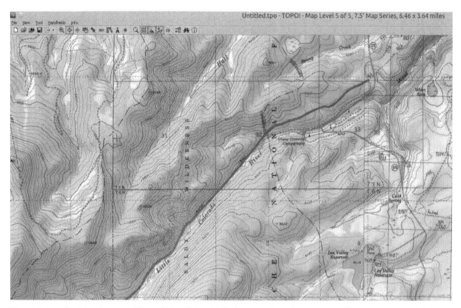

Drawing a freehand route (the solid red line) along a trail with TOPO!, ©2010 National Geographic

Drawing a Freehand Route

Because this hike will follow trails, we will plan the route using the Topo! route tool, which allows you to trace freehand routes. After zooming in to Level 5 in the area of Mount Baldy, select "Tools | Route" from the Topo! menu. Draw a freehand route from the starting point to the ending point of the hike, following the trails as closely as possible. Our hike will start at Sheep Crossing Trailhead, follow the West Baldy Trail to the summit area, descend via the East Baldy Trail, and then close the loop by using the Connector Trail. The new Sheep Crossing Trailhead and the upper parts of the West and East Baldy trails have been relocated and are not shown on the topo, and the relatively new Connector Trail is not shown at all. Information on the trails is available from the U.S. Forest Service Web site and from hiking guidebooks. We'll deal with this as it affects our GPS route in the next chapter.

This route is a loop, so stop drawing just short of the starting point. On a loop route such as this, it is a good idea to keep the start and end of the loop slightly separated, because the GPS receiver can get confused and start navigating the wrong way around the loop. Now, right-click on the route, and change the style and color of the route line to thin dashed blue. Topo! uses red by default for both freehand routes and GPS routes, so changing the color and style of the freehand route makes it stand out from the GPS route we are about to create.

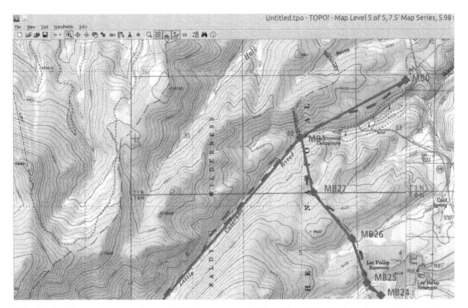

The freehand route converted to a GPS route as a solid red line. The freehand route is the blue dashed line. TOPO!, ©2010 National Geographic

We are going to create the GPS route from the freehand route. To do this, right-click anywhere on the freehand route, and select "GPS Route" from the Route Editor dialog box. The GPS Route Name Editor should pop up, allowing you to name the loop MTBALDY. If the editor doesn't appear, name the route later by right-clicking on it with the GPS Waypoint tool. Next, the GPS Route Wizard will appear. You'll need to select the number of waypoints you want the wizard to create along the route. The number depends on the length and complexity of the route, so you'll have to experiment to see what works. If you mess up, just delete the GPS route and waypoints and make a new GPS route from the freehand route, using the Route tool as before. In this case, we'll ask the wizard to make 30 waypoints. Make certain "Match the shape of the freehand route as closely as possible" is selected, and then type a short prefix in the box, in this case "MB". This prefix will be added to the automatic waypoint names, so that they are unique and won't conflict with the waypoints for the next route we're going to plan. Click "Finish" and Topo! creates your route. From the menu, select "File | Save As" and name the file "MountBaldyLoop". This saves your work as a TPO file.

Printing Maps

In most cases, you'll want to print the map for use on the trip. To do this in Topo!, select "File | Print" from the menu, or click the "Print or Export" tool on the toolbar. A red rectangle appears on the map showing the area that will print. You can left-click and drag the print rectangle to cover the desired area, and resize it by left-clicking and dragging the borders. Other options on the print tab at the right side of the screen let you set the map scale and decide which map features to print, such as elevation profiles. For long trips, you'll have to print several pages to show the entire route. It helps to number the printouts in order so they're easier to find on the trip.

Maps can be printed on ink jet and laser printers. Ink jet maps show the most detail and can be printed in color, but are not waterproof unless printed on special paper. Monochrome and color laser printouts are more water resistant, but all printed maps should be carried in a zipper plastic bag or a map case to protect them from damp conditions.

Finding a Baseline

Part of your planning should include locating a "baseline". A baseline is an unmistakable landmark, such as a road, major trail, or a river, that runs along one side of the area you plan to explore. In the unlikely event that you get totally disoriented and lost, you can always hike to your baseline. In this case, the access road to the trailhead, State 273, runs along the east side of the Mount Baldy area and makes a perfect baseline.

Planning a Cross-Country Ski

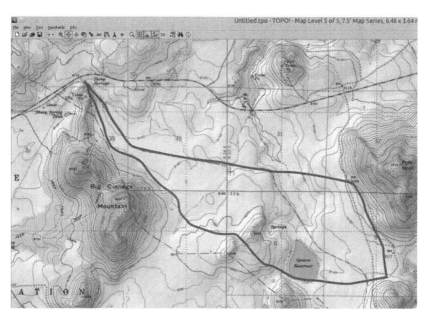

Using Topo! to draw a freehand cross-country route. TOPO!, ©2010 National Geographic

Drawing a Freehand Cross-Country Ski Route

We're going to plan a ski route in the alpine meadows of Arizona's White Mountains. Zoom in to Level 5 in the area of the trip, which will start from the 260 Trailhead on State 260. Using the Route Tool as we did in the last example, draw a freehand route from the trailhead to a point just short of the trailhead on the return. Again, right-click on the route and change the color and style of the route to blue thin dashed. Right-click on the route and select GPS Route from the Route Editor dialog. In the GPS Route Name Editor, name the loop "260SKI".

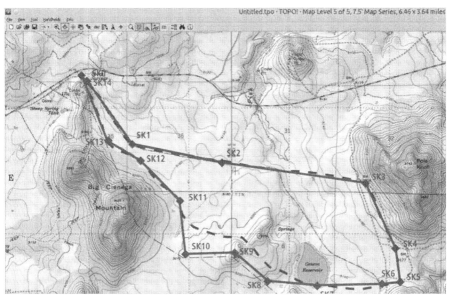

The GPS route created from the freehand route after moving several waypoints. TOPO!,
©2010 National Geographic

With the GPS Route Wizard, create 15 waypoints and enter the prefix "SK". Make certain "Match the shape of the freehand route as closely as possible" is selected. Click "Finish" to create the GPS route. As before, if you don't like the GPS route, you can delete it and start over.

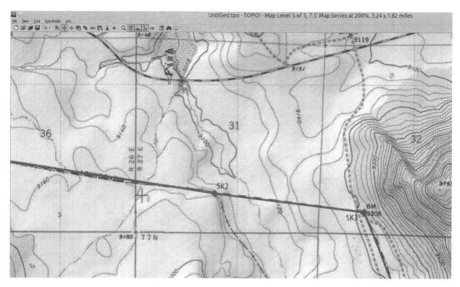

Moving a waypoint. TOPO!, ©2010 National Geographic

Editing the Waypoints

If you aren't happy with the placement of a waypoint, you can left-click and drag it to a new location, and the route will move as well. In this case, we are following the Apache Railroad Trail for the first part of the ski tour. SK2 is along a straight portion of the historic railroad grade, but we want to leave the railroad grade at the sharp bend in the middle of the meadow. So, drag SK2 over to the bend. Toward the end of the loop, we want to ski closer to the boundary between the Apache National Forest and the Fort Apache Indian Reservation, so we move SK8, SK9, and SK10 over to the boundary. The reservation is closed to public access, so the GPS receiver will be very useful in keeping our party legal and on the national forest.

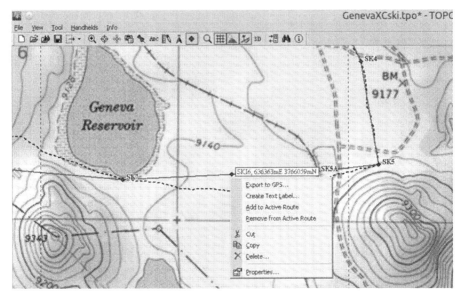

Deleting a waypoint. TOPO!, ©2010 National Geographic

You can delete any waypoint by right-clicking on it with the GPS Waypoint tool and selecting "Delete". When prompted, delete the waypoint from the file as well. In this case, SK6 seems unnecessary, so delete it.

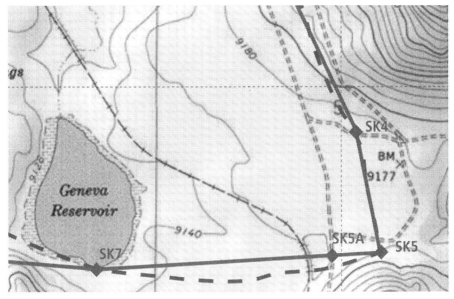

Adding a waypoint. TOPO!, ©2010 National Geographic

To insert a new waypoint along the route, left-click anywhere along the route line. In this case, we decide we want a new waypoint between SK5 and SK7 where our route crosses the Apache Railroad Trail. Name the inserted waypoint "SK5A" to make it clear the waypoint is between SK5 and SK7.

You can create a waypoint that is not part of your route by right-clicking on the route with the GPS Waypoint tool and selecting "Deactivate this route". The route turns blue to show that it is deactivated. Next, left-click anywhere on the map to create a new waypoint. We decide that we might want to check out the springs northwest of Geneva Reservoir, so we create a waypoint there and name it "SKSPRING".

We're happy with the route now, so we export it to the GPS receiver. This time, we want to export "All routes and waypoints" to make certain we export the inactive route as well as the independent waypoint.

Planning a Paddle

We're going to plan a day trip by sea kayak on Utah's Lake Powell using Topo! The plan is to start at the boat ramp at Wahweap Marina and paddle to some interesting canyons along the west side of Romana Mesa. To start, zoom in to level 5 at Wahweap Marina at the west end of Lake Powell. From the menu, select "Hand Helds | New GPS Route".

Because we'll be paddling this route in straight line segments, we're going to build this GPS route by left-clicking on the map to manually create waypoints. As you create waypoints, they are added to the route in sequence and a red line on the map shows the route. Name the waypoints using a name that relates to their location, if possible. Again, start each waypoint with a couple of letters- in this case "LP" to ensure the waypoints have unique names.

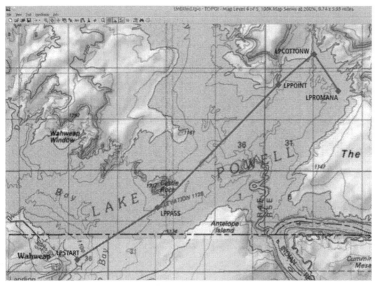

The paddle route on Lake Powell. TOPO!, ©2010 National Geographic

The first waypoint, LPSTART, is at the Wahweap Marina boat ramp, our launch point. The second waypoint, LPPASS, is at the pass south of Castle Rock, which is narrow and difficult to spot from a kayak at lower lake levels. (Checking the current Lake Powell water level on the Web, we learn that it is at 3637 feet, 63 feet below maximum.) LPANTELOPE is at the north tip of Antelope Island at this water level. LPPOINT marks the end of the long crossing from LPPASS and LPCOTTONW marks the entrance to Cottonwood Canyon, the first canyon you want to check out. Finally LPROMANA marks the last, unnamed, canyon that you want to explore. Save the file and export it to the GPS receiver. Also, print the map from Topo! for use on the trip. We'll navigate this trip in the next chapter.

Finding Trips Online

One of the greatest things about GPS is that you can let someone else do some of the planning by downloading trips from the Web. Most of these sites also let you upload trips and share them with others, the subject of the chapter Share Your Trip. The common file format for GPS waypoints, routes, and tracks is GPX, which most sites and applications support. These Web sites are changing rapidly, and some of them are a bit rough around the edges. Also, most of the sites depend on user reviews to determine the accuracy and quality of the trip, so, like anything on the Web, be skeptical. It's a good idea to cross-check the information with someone who's been there, such as an experienced friend or a ranger. Some of the sites that are currently available:

> www.backpacker.com/destinations/ is a site developed by Backpacker Magazine in conjunction with Trimble Outdoors. It features trips uploaded and rated by the magazine staff, readers, and other sources. You can download trips to your computer in GPX format, and also to the iPhone, Android-based phones, web account, and Google Earth.

> www.everytrail.com has a growing collection of trips uploaded and rated by users, including road, trail, and water trips. You can upload and download trips via email, instant messaging, GPX files, and Google Earth KML files.

> Google Earth (http://earth.google.com/) is a free application that runs on Mac, PC, and Linux and has detailed satellite imagery of the entire planet. Downloading trip data can only be done in Google Earth's KML or KMZ formats. You'll have to use a program such as GPS Babel to convert to GPX format and open the GPX file in Easy GPS, Topo!, Garmin MapSource, or another GPX-friendly program in order to import it to your GPS receiver.

> National Geographic Topo! Explorer (www.topo.com) is an online version of National Geographic Topo! with added trip sharing features. You can use existing Topo! State Series maps if you have them or download "Superquads" at additional cost.

> Trimble Outdoors (www.trimbleoutdoors.com) has trips uploaded and rated by users. Trips can be downloaded to your computer in GPX format and Google Earth in KML format. You can also plan your own trip online.

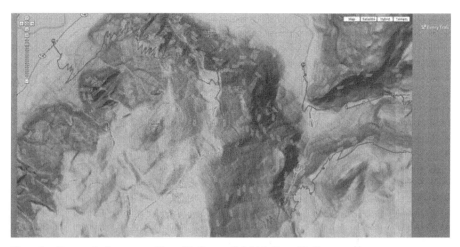

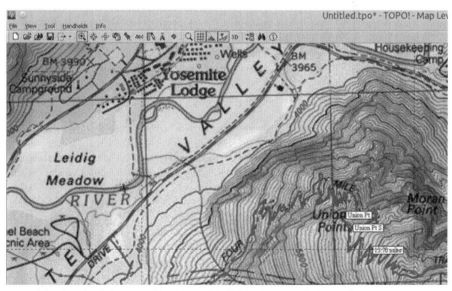

41

Downloading a Trip From www.EveryTrail.com

Search or browse by location or activity to find the trip you want, then download the GPX file to your computer by clicking on "Download GPX for your GPS". This link is located on the right side under "Export This Trip." After the file has finished downloading, open Topo! (or start with a new map if Topo! is already open), and select "Hand Helds | Import (from GPS or text) Wizard". From the Import Wizard, select "In a .gpx file...". Note: Some GPX files may have waypoints that are too long for your GPS. You can either rename them yourself, or let Topo! do it for you. After the trip has been imported, you can work with the waypoints, GPS routes, and freehand routes using all of the tools in Topo! You can then export the route to your GPS.

On the Road

Driving to the Sheep Trail with Trail GPS

In this section, we'll use the route created for your trail GPS in the previous chapter to navigate to the Sheep Trail trailhead on the Navajo Indian Reservation.

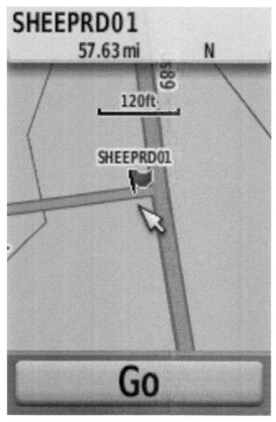

Starting "Go To" navigation to the SHEEPRD01 waypoint at the highway turnoff on a Garmin trail GPS

Navigating to the Turnoff

The first problem is to find the highway turnoff. As mentioned earlier, many of the dirt roads on the Indian reservation are not marked. When we created the SHEEPROAD route from the highway to the trailhead, we started by creating a waypoint at the turnoff. We can use that waypoint to find the turnoff by navigating a "Go To" route.

"Go To" Routes

The method used to select a waypoint for direct, "Go To" navigation varies on different trail GPS receivers. Some units have a Find button, while on others you'll select Waypoints from a menu. On mapping receivers, you can also go to the map screen and pan the map to select a waypoint. In this case, we are navigating directly to the SHEEPRD01 waypoint. You may be asked whether to follow roads or go off road. Select "Off Road". If you have street mapping installed on your trail GPS, you can select "Follow Road" and navigate to the turnoff just as you would on a street GPS. If you don't have street mapping, or you select "Off Road", then the GPS receiver creates a route directly from your present position to SHEEPRD01. In this case, "Off Road" is fine because we already know how to drive out of town and find U.S. 89 northbound.

You can use "Go To" navigation to go directly to any waypoint in your GPS receiver. This is a very handy capability and one that you'll use often.

In either navigation mode, the GPS will beep and/or pop up a message on the screen as you approach the turn off. After you make the turn off the highway, stop for a moment and mark a waypoint at the turnoff as a backup. Also make sure the track log is on and set to "AUTO". This lets you create a backtrack route if necessary. Next, you'll activate the SHEEPROAD route.

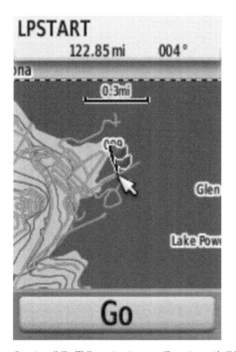 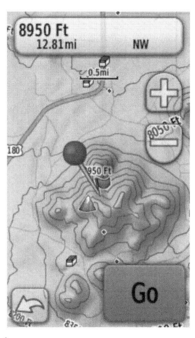

Starting "Go To" navigation on Garmin trail GPS receivers

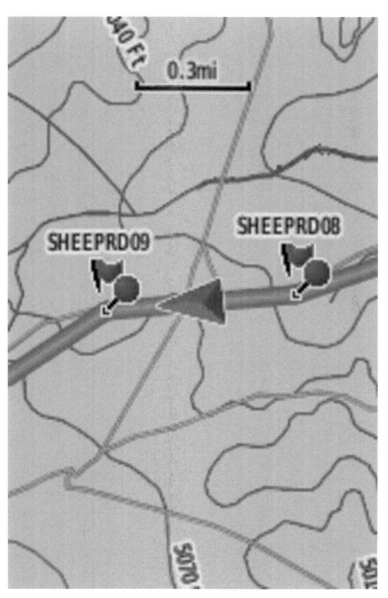

Navigating the SHEEPROAD route using the map page on a Garmin trail GPS

Following the SHEEPROAD Route

To activate a route on most trail GPS units, go to the main menu and select Routes. Then pick the desired route from the list. In this case, we are going to navigate the SHEEPROAD route we planned in the last chapter.

You'll probably find the map page the most useful for following back roads on a trail GPS. In this example, we'll use the waypoints as a general guide to the trailhead. We know that our destination, the waypoint at the trailhead, is accurate because we verified the trailhead from a guidebook description and Google Earth.

The approach road heads generally west to the SHEEPRD12 waypoint, and then heads more or less south to the north rim of the Little Colorado River Gorge and the trailhead. As you approach each waypoint, the GPS receiver beeps and/or displays a message. Watch for the intersection and take the fork that heads toward the next waypoint as shown on the GPS map. Even if the waypoint isn't quite on the road, the map page should give you an idea how to proceed. If you take a road that starts heading the wrong direction, the GPS map will soon make this apparent so you can backtrack. If you reach an intersection with no waypoint, look at the map page and try to turn toward the next waypoint. Using this method, the GPS receiver saves a vast amount of time compared to the traditional navigation method of using landmarks to find your position on a topo map.

Continue using this procedure with your GPS until you reach the trailhead. Now, before you start hiking, save a waypoint at the trailhead and save the track log. When you return to your vehicle you can create a backtrack route, as described earlier, and use it to navigate precisely to the highway. As you proceed, any false turns you made will be apparent on the map page.

Hitting the Trail

The West Baldy Trail follows alpine meadows along the West Fork of the Little Colorado River. The trail has been rerouted in several places and is not shown correctly on the topo map.

In this example, we'll follow the MTBALDY route we created in the previous chapter. We'll also do some trail mapping.

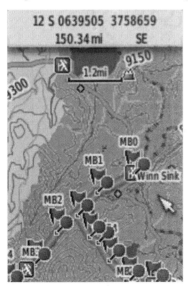

The MTBALDY route on the map page of a Garmin trail GPS

At the Trailhead

Before leaving the car, do the standard GPS procedure:

- Get a solid satellite fix

- Mark the trailhead location as a waypoint

- Make sure the track log is on

On this hike, which involves a climb over the summit of Mount Baldy, we want to track elevation changes on the GPS receiver. To do this on a trail GPS unit, go to the altimeter page, press "MENU" and select "Reset" to clear old elevation data. Next, the barometric altimeter must be calibrated by entering either your elevation or the current barometer setting for your location. In this case, we can set the altimeter to the elevation of the trailhead, 9,770 feet, as read from our printed topo map. From the menu, select "Calibrate" and follow the instructions. Finally, go to the routes page and activate the "MTBALDY" route.

There are two ways you can use your GPS on a hike or other backcountry trip where you do not have vehicle power to run your GPS. You can keep the GPS turned off most of the time and turn it on when you want to check your progress and see how far it is to the next waypoint. Or you can keep it turned on for constant reference, and more importantly, to record a track log and save waypoints. With fully charged NiMH batteries or fresh lithium single-use batteries, most GPS receivers will last for a full day. But always carry at least one set of spare batteries. On a backpack trip, you may have no choice but to keep the unit off most of the time. Doing this will extend the GPS battery life to days rather than hours.

On this example trip, which is a long day hike, we will keep the GPS turned on because we want to map the trail. We happen to know that the trail has been relocated by the U.S. Forest Service since the topo maps were last updated. Also, there's an ongoing controversy involving the Fort Apache Indian Reservation boundary. The boundary runs along the Mount Baldy summit ridge and hikers have been fined for entering the reservation without a permit. On this hike, we want to map the trail accurately and verify that it stays off the reservation and on the Apache National Forest. We also want to determine if the highest point of Mount Baldy is on the forest or the reservation.

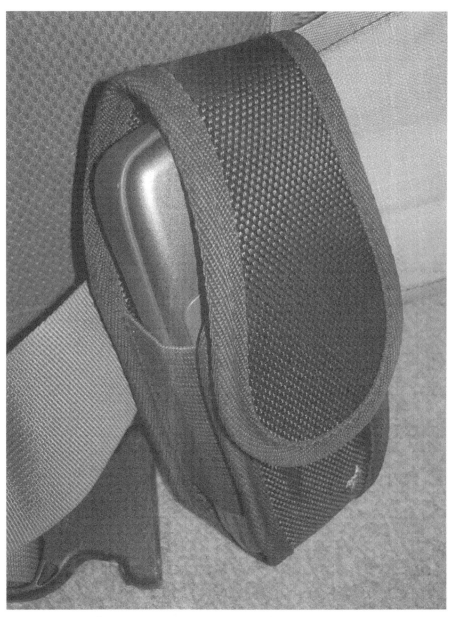

GPS receiver carried in a Nite Ize case on the pack hipbelt

You'll need to carry the GPS receiver where you can get it easily while hiking, and where it has a decent view of the sky. Modern units with high sensitivity receivers usually keep a satellite lock when carried on a pack shoulder strap or on a hip belt. Nite Ize (www.niteize.com) makes a line of rugged holsters that have a rotatable and secure mounting clip.

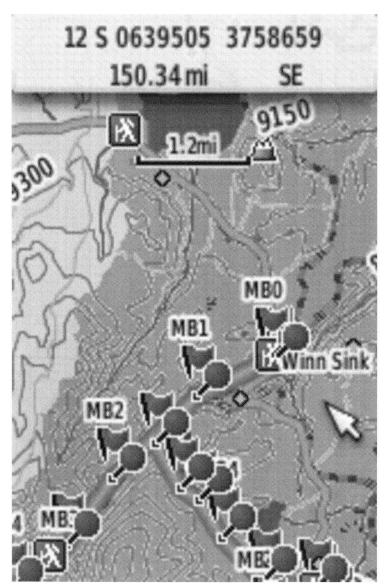

The map page on a Garmin trail GPS showing the first part of the Mount Baldy loop

On the Trail

When hiking a trail, you'll probably find the map page to be the most useful. As you walk, you can periodically check the GPS to see how you are progressing toward the next waypoint. The data field at the top of the page shows the direction and distance to the next waypoint.

Mapping a Trail with GPS

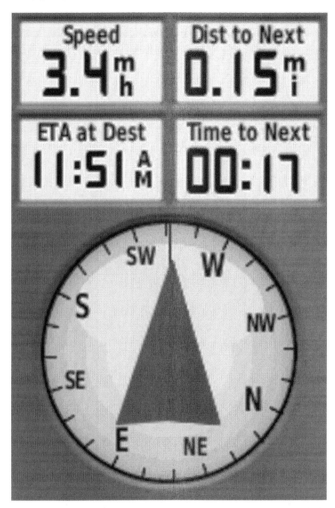

Checking your progress with the compass page on a Garmin trail GPS

You can also use the compass page to check your progress. On most trail GPS receivers, the default data fields show your speed, the distance to the next waypoint, the time to the next waypoint, and the estimated time of arrival (ETA) at your destination. When hiking, use this information with caution as civilian GPS receivers are not precise enough to compute speed accurately at walking speeds. This is because the unit uses a series of position fixes to compute your speed. Because the accuracy of civilian GPS is 10 meters (33 feet), the position fixes have slight errors which accumulate as you travel. At walking speeds, my field tests with trail GPS receivers have shown speed and distance errors of about 5%. At higher speeds, such as paddling a canoe or riding a bicycle, the error is not as much of a factor and GPS time, distance, and speed are accurate enough for outdoor use.

An easy way to demonstrate these low speed distance errors is to turn your GPS receiver on, reset the odometer data, and leave it stationary. After an hour or two, the odometer page on the GPS receiver will accumulate a significant distance traveled, even though the unit hasn't moved at all.

Rangers and other professional field users of GPS use differential GPS (DGPS) to accurately measure distance with a precision of a few centimeters or less. With DGPS, time and speed can be measured very accurately at walking speeds. See the The Complete Navigator chapter for more information.

Another reason that the distance and time information on the GPS may be off when hiking a trail is that the GPS route doesn't follow the trail exactly, so the trail is always a little longer than the GPS route. You can see this on the Map screen as you hike. The track log that is created as you move is shown on the Map screen as a faint line of dots, so you can compare that with the straight segments of the preloaded GPS route. As with speed, expect your actual distances and times to be as much as 5% longer than the GPS data. A much more accurate way to measure trail distance is to import the GPS track log into a program such as National Geographic Topo! or DeLorme Topo North America and create an elevation profile of the track. This method averages out the errors and also accounts for climbs and descents. My tests have shown errors of 2% or less as compared to measurements with a calibrated bicycle cyclometer. See Measuring Trail Distance with Tracks for details.

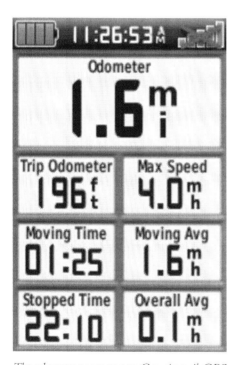 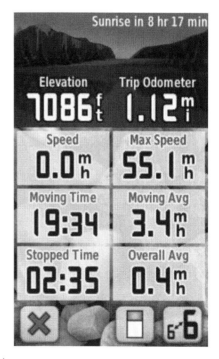

The odometer pages on two Garmin trail GPS receivers

The odometer page displays a trip odometer (distance you've traveled on this trip), as well as related information such as your maximum speed, moving time, moving average speed, stopped time, overall average speed, elevation, and an overall odometer. All these data fields can be reset to zero at the start of your hike. Because of the limitations discussed above, the most useful field for the hiker is overall average speed. As you'll see in the next section, the odometer page is more helpful for paddlers who are moving at a higher speed and along more direct routes. Cyclists also find the odometer page useful.

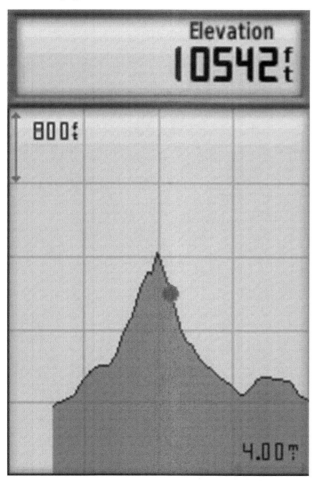

The altimeter page on a Garmin trail GPS showing an elevation graph

On most trail GPS receivers, the altimeter page can be used as you travel to show a graph of your route's elevation profile. The default page also shows your total ascent, maximum elevation, rate of ascent or descent, and the current elevation. The altimeter page can also be used to monitor changes in the barometric pressure while you are not moving, such as in camp, to watch for changes in the weather. See the The Complete Navigator chapter for more information.

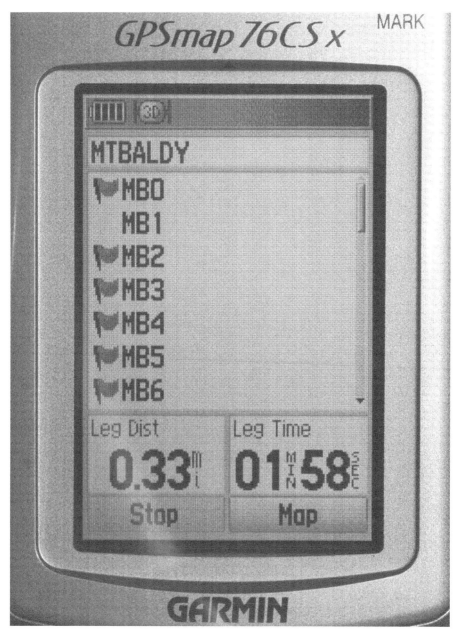

The active route page enroute to MB1 on a Garmin trail GPS

As you progress, the active route page shows where you are along the GPS route by flashing the symbol to the left of the next waypoint. Using this page, you can review, insert, remove, change, or move waypoints in the active route. You can also create an elevation profile of the route.

Marking the actual location of the Connector Trail junction as waypoint 002 on a Garmin trail GPS

As mentioned earlier, one of your objectives on this hike is to accurately map the trails. The track log does this automatically as you hike, but you'll still want to mark important locations along the trail, such as springs, points of interest, and trail junctions. When you save a waypoint on a GPS receiver, the unit assigns a default waypoint name, such as 002. You can change the name and add a comment, but it's time consuming to do this on the GPS unit in the field. A much easier way to is take notes on each field waypoint in a small notebook or with a pocket voice recorder. Many digital recorders have a USB connection so you can transfer your field notes to your computer back at home. The recorder is also useful for taking notes on photos or video that you shoot on the hike.

The first waypoint on the preplanned route is MB1, which should mark the intersection with the north end of the Connector Trail. Because the trail is not shown on the topo map, you could only locate it approximately from a guidebook description. Now you've arrived at MB1 but there's no trail junction. You keep hiking and discover the junction about a quarter mile farther on. Mark this junction, which will be waypoint 002 if you started with 001 at the trailhead, and note the name and purpose of the waypoint in your trail notes.

Updating your route by changing MB1 to 002 on a Garmin trail GPS

Updating Your Route

Since the Connector Trail will be your return route, you'll want to change the MB1 waypoint in the MTBALDY route to the 002 waypoint. To do this, go to the active route page, scroll down to MB1, and press "ENTER". From the pop-up menu, select "Change". Then choose the 002 waypoint from the waypoint page and select "Use". This replaces MB1 with 002, the actual location of the Connector Trail junction.

As you hike the rest of the trail to Mount Baldy, mark new waypoints as needed. You don't have to update the MTBALDY route in the field after MB1, because you won't be retracing your steps. You would update the route if this was an out-and-back hike.

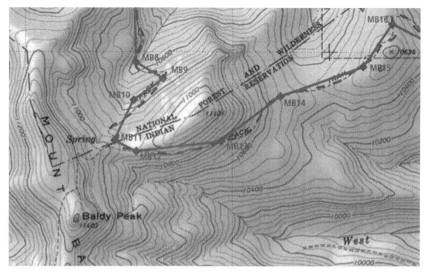

The trail and preplanned GPS route near the summit of Mount Baldy. TOPO!, ©2010 National Geographic

Checking the Trail Location on Mount Baldy

Sure enough, you find that beyond the MB4 waypoint the West Baldy Trail has been significantly rerouted. It skirts the north side of the meadow at the head of the West Fork and then appears to climb up the north slope of the northeast ridge of Mount Baldy. Of course, you follow the new trail instead of the obviously incorrect GPS route you planned at home. You zoom in on the map page to verify this. You also save waypoints at each turn or switchback in the trail to back up the track log. A series of switchbacks eventually bring the trail up to the north end of the summit ridge, marked "MOUNT BALDY" on the printed Topo! map.

Hikers have gotten into trouble with the Fort Apache Tribe by illegally hiking to Baldy Peak, the named 11,403-foot summit at the south end of the "Mount Baldy" summit ridge. From your study of the topo map before the trip, it was obvious that Baldy Peak is well onto the reservation, because the forest/reservation boundary turns sharply east well north of Baldy Peak. However, the highest portion of the summit ridge itself is enclosed by an 11,400-foot contour line. When you were planning the trip at home, you used the mouse cursor in Topo! to measure the highest point within the 11,400-foot contour and came up with 11,412 feet, which would make the Mount Baldy summit ridge the actual high point of the mountain. You also noticed that the reservation boundary doesn't run along the actual crest of the ridge. Instead the boundary is located slightly west of the crest along the 11,400-foot contour line. Now, this all seems nit-picky, except that you know Mount Baldy is popular with peak-bagging hikers. That desire has gotten numerous hikers in trouble with the tribe, who often station a ranger just out of sight below Baldy Peak. (The reservation does not issue hiking permits for their portion of Mount Baldy, which is closed to the public.)

Mount Baldy summit ridge, looking south. The reservation boundary runs along the right side of the ridge, just below the crest.

The Forest Service trail stays well below the summit ridge on its east side, near the tree line, and is marked with National Forest boundary signs. Because you suspect the signs are wrong, you walk up to the north end of the summit ridge. Sure enough, you spot a line of metal survey caps just below the ridge crest on the west, and follow them to the south end of the summit ridge, where they turn abruptly east. This physical evidence confirms your theory that the reservation boundary is just west of the actual high point of the mountain, which is near the "O" in "MOUNT BALDY" on the topo. You save a waypoint on the GPS at the exact spot.

After that discovery, the rest of the hike is fairly routine, as you descend along the East Fork Trail following the GPS route. You do find that the upper part of the trail has also been rerouted to keep it out of the reservation, so you save waypoints at the key points. You also discover an old airplane wreck, which you mark with the GPS.

Importing Your Field GPS Data to the Computer

Back home, hook up your GPS receiver to the computer. In Topo!, select "Hand Helds | Import (from GPS or text file) Wizard", then "In a GPS receiver..." In the next dialog box, check "Waypoints", "Routes", and "Tracks (make a freehand route...)". Make sure "NAD83 or WGS 84..." is checked, then click "Finish". The GPS data will be imported to Topo! Now you can work with it on the computer, which is much easier than working with it on the GPS receiver. For example, you can rename the field waypoints (001, 002, etc.) to something meaningful and add waypoint comments. I save Topo! files with GPS data recorded in the field with a name ending in "field" so I can distinguish these files from preplanned route files.

Snow Bound

Winter at the 260 Trailhead

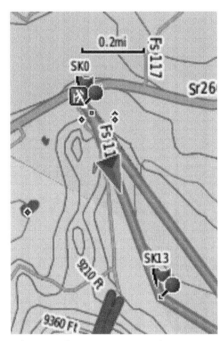

The reversed 260SKI route on the map page of a Garmin trail GPS

In this chapter we'll ski the route we planned in the "Plan Ahead" chapter. Arriving at the 260 Trailhead, you and the group decide to ski the route in reverse because the weather looks threatening. That will keep you nearer the forest, at least at the start of the ski, if the wind picks up. After doing the standard trailhead items on your GPS (getting a 4-satellite fix, marking the trailhead, and turning on the track log), go to the routes page. Select the route 260SKI and press "ENTER". To reverse the route, press "MENU" and select "Reverse Route". Then press "ENTER" twice to reverse the route and activate navigation.

Checking Your Position

Since you're not following a trail on the first part of the loop and you can see where you're going, you decide to turn the GPS receiver off while you ski. You'll check your position when you stop for a break.

On the first leg, on the way to waypoint SK13, you ski up to a fence that appears to mark the reservation boundary. Since you don't want to trespass, you switch on the GPS. Because you just used it at the trailhead, the receiver gets a 4-satellite fix in seconds. Zooming in on the map page, you see that the reservation boundary is shown on the GPS topo map and verify that the fence is the boundary. You switch the GPS off and keep skiing. Periodically you stop, turn the GPS receiver on, and check your progress. Each time you do this, the unit shows your progress along the 260SKI route. From SK10 to SKI8, you're skiing along the reservation boundary fence, but then you and your group strike out east for the south side of Geneva Reservoir.

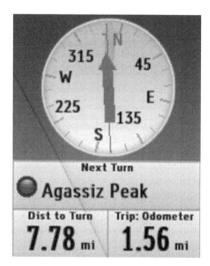

The compass pages on Garmin and DeLorme trail GPS receivers

White Out!

The trip is uneventful until you are skiing along the base of Pole Knoll, between SK4 and SK3. Snow starts to fall thickly from the heavy overcast, and soon visibility is only a couple of hundred feet. At SK3, your group takes shelter in the forest at the edge of the meadow to make plans. You know that a graded forest road runs along the west side of Pole Knoll and reaches Highway 260 less than a mile north of your present position. On the other hand, there's no real reason to bail out. Your group has good windproof clothing in case the wind picks up on the open crossing back to the trailhead. You decide to continue along the 260SKI route in reverse as originally planned. You could go directly to the trailhead, but it wouldn't be that much shorter and the skiing may be easier along the Apache Railroad Trail.

Since you can't ski and hold the GPS in your hand, you leave it on and carry it in a case on your belt. To maintain the correct course without landmarks, you put an experienced skier about 100 feet in front. The less- experienced skiers are close behind you, followed by another experienced skier to make sure no one strays. As you travel, you occasionally pull out the GPS and check your course on the compass page. The bearing pointer clearly shows which way to turn to head to the next waypoint. Then you call out directions to the lead skier to turn slightly right or left, as needed. It's eerie out in the meadow surrounded by swirling white, but the GPS receiver is not affected by the weather and stays reliably locked on to the satellites. You ski up a slight hill approaching SK2 and sure enough, ski onto the old railroad grade right at the bend, where the wind has blown the snow off the embankment. On the flat, the trail disappears under the snow drifts, but no matter. The GPS takes your group right to the 260 Trailhead and the yummy thermos of hot chocolate you left in your car.

On the Water

Sea kayaking on Lake Powell

We're going to navigate the LPROMANA route on Lake Powell that we put together in the "Plan Ahead" chapter. This will show how the use of GPS differs when you travel straight line routes, as opposed to following trails and roads.

Setting off to paddle the LPROMANA route, as shown on the map page of a Garmin trail GPS

At the Put-In

When you arrive at the starting point at the Wahweap Marina boat ramp, turn on your GPS and do the standard trailhead routine on your GPS (getting a 4-satellite fix, marking the boat launch, and turning on the track log.)

When you are ready to leave the launch site, go to the routes page and activate the LPROMANA route. The route will be shown on the map page with the name of the next waypoint at the top. On the compass page, the bearing pointer will show the direction you need to paddle to reach LPPASS, the first waypoint on the route. The active route page will show a list of the waypoints on the route and the symbol to the left of the next waypoint will flash.

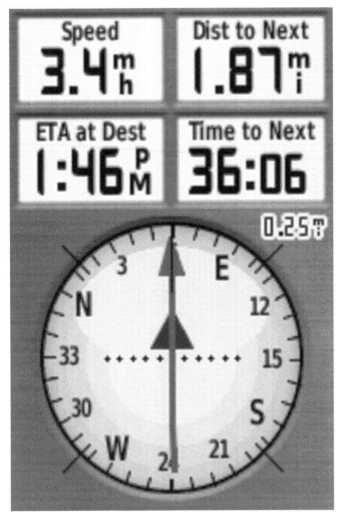

Compass page with course pointer on a Garmin trail GPS

Blowing in the Wind

You have the GPS in a waterproof deck bag mounted on the kayak deck in front of the cockpit so you can easily refer to it as you paddle. You could use the bearing pointer on the compass page to keep heading toward the next waypoint, but the bearing pointer doesn't show how far off course you are. Since you might find yourself being pushed off course by wind or current, you decide to use the course pointer. To do this on the compass page, press the "MENU" button and select "Course Pointer". Now, the red arrow on the compass page is flanked on either side by five small dots, each of which represent 0.25-mile off course. As you paddle, the middle part of the course pointer becomes a separate bar that moves to one side if you get off course. To get back on course, turn toward the offset bar. This way, you can leave the map zoomed out so you can see the overall navigation picture, and use the compass page to stay on course. With a bit of trial and error, you'll find out how much you have to keep your bow turned toward the wind or into the offsetting current to stay on course.

The compass page also shows your speed, the estimated time of arrival (ETA) at your destination, and the distance and time to the next waypoint, LPPASS.

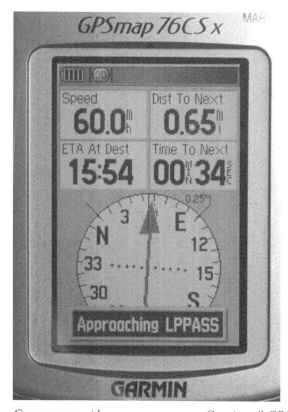

Compass page with pop-up message on a Garmin trail GPS

As you approach the LPPASS waypoint, the receiver beeps and/or a message pops up showing that you are nearing the waypoint. When you reach the waypoint, the course pointer moves to show the new direction to paddle. As before, turn until the pointer is lined up with the lubber line at the top of the compass. The map and active route pages now show that the next waypoint is LPPOINT. As you paddle, use the course pointer on the compass page to stay on course as you did on the previous leg.

After reaching LPCOTTONW, your party lands in the mouth of Cottonwood Canyon to have a snack and check out the canyon. Back on the water, you work your way along the base of Romana Mesa, checking out canyons that look interesting. When you reach the last canyon, the unnamed canyon at LPROMANA, it's time to head back to the boat ramp.

Going Direct

Rather than retracing your route, you want to save time by paddling directly back to the pass at LPPASS. To do this, press "FIND", select "Waypoints", and then select "LPPASS". Press "ENTER" to activate a "Go To" route to LPPASS. Now you can paddle directly to the hidden pass. Once through the pass, do another "Go To" route directly to LPSTART.

Share Your Trip

Sharing trips online lets others use your GPS data for their own trips, as well as see your notes, comments, photos, and videos. You can easily email TPO and GPX files to friends, or you can upload your trip to one of the trip sharing Web sites, an activity that is starting to be called "E-Hiking." See Finding Trips Online for a current list of trip-sharing Web sites.

For more information on trip sharing and E-Hiking, refer to my other book, *Using a GPS: Digital Trip Planning, Recording, and Sharing*, published by The Globe Pequot Press and Backpacker Magazine.

Email

To email GPS trip data to a friend using National Geographic Topo!, just save the trip as a TPO or GPX file. Since TPO files only work with Topo!, you should use GPX unless you know the recipient has Topo! GPX is rapidly becoming the standard file format for GPS waypoints, routes, and tracks. Most digital mapping programs, as well as Google Earth, can import GPX files. You can also use a free program such as GPS Babel to download GPS data directly from your GPS receiver to a GPX file. Unfortunately, all you can share in this way is the GPS data. If you want to share photos, comments, or video, you'll have to attach the files separately.

Web

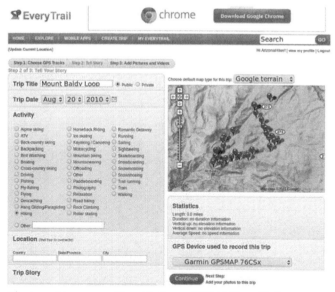

Sharing a trip on www.EveryTrail.com. ©2010 EveryTrail.com

On the Web, you can share not only the GPS data, you can also attach comments, other trip data, photos, and video to a trip, depending on the site. For example, at www.everytrail.com you can upload a GPX file to create a map of the trip, then add a description of the trip. You can upload photos from your computer, or import photos or video from Flickr, Picasa, or YouTube. Other users of the site can comment on your trip and rate it.

Treasure Hunting

Aside from using GPS to support a wide range of traditional outdoor recreational activities from hiking to hunting, the advent of GPS has been the catalyst for several new outdoor pursuits, including geocaching, benchmarking, and waymarking.

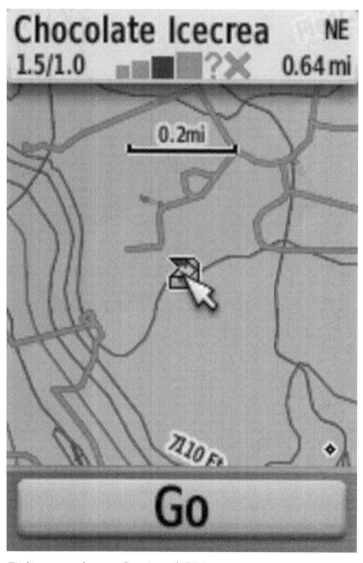

Finding a geocache on a Garmin trail GPS

Geocaching

Geocaching is a modern version of treasure hunting with assistance from GPS. Geocachers hunt for small containers that are hidden outdoors, in rural areas as well as cities, and then log their discovery online. The most popular meeting place for geocachers worldwide is the Groundspeak Web site, www.geocaching.com. There are currently well over a million active geocaches on the site and more than five million geocachers worldwide.

An alternative, non-commercial site, www.opencaching.com, is supported by the geocaching community and sponsored by Garmin.

Finding a Geocache Near You

On geocaching.com, you can search for geocaches by address, postal code, state/province, country, latitude and longitude, keyword, geocache code, and geocache.com username. Then, you can download a GPX file and use a program such as EasyGps (www.easygps.com) to export the data to your GPS. Users of Garmin GPS units can transfer geocaches directly to their receiver with the use of a free Garmin plugin downloaded from www8.garmin.com/products/communicator/.

Navigating to a geocache with the map page on a Garmin trail GPS

The Hunt

Once the geocache is stored in your GPS receiver, you can navigate to it just as you do any other waypoint. You'll probably want to print the geocache details to take along, since GPS will only get you within about 30 feet. Many geocachers provide additional clues if the geocache is well hidden.

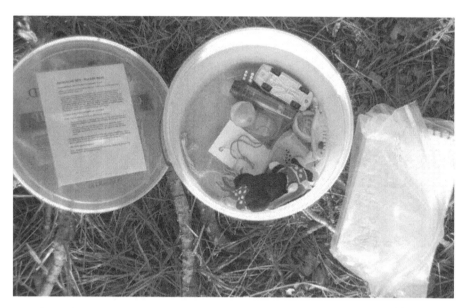

A traditional geocache containing small treasure objects. On the right, there's a notebook in a plastic bag for recording your comments. On the left, taped to the lid, there's an explanation of the geocache.

The Cache

There are many different types of geocache. For details, visit www.opencaching.com. The most common types:

- Traditional Cache: The original geocache having a container and log book. Some caches have small objects (the "treasure"), the idea being that you take something and leave something.

- Multi-Cache: Caches with several locations, the first giving clues to the second, the second to the third, and so on to the final cache. An Offset Cache is a variation where the first cache gives directions to the final cache.

- Mystery Cache: Requires solving a puzzle to determine the coordinates of the cache.

- Letterbox Hybrid: A letterbox uses clues instead of coordinates, and a hybrid uses both. For more about letterboxing visit the Letterboxing North America Web site, www.letterboxing.org.

Logging Your Find

Back home, you can go on www.geocaching.com or www.opencaching.com and log your find, as well as read about other people's experiences with the cache. To log your find, you'll need to sign up for a free account, which also gives you more options for downloading caches. Active geocachers may want to sign up for a paid premium account, which allows access to advanced features such as batch downloading of geocache data. Either type of account also gives access to www.waymarking.com, the waymarking Web site also owned by Groundspeak.

Ground Rules

- If you take something from a cache, leave something of equal value
- Don't leave hazardous objects in a cache. Geocachers are all ages, children to adults
- Don't put food in a cache. Animals will inevitably find and destroy the cache
- Never move a cache

Geocache icon on the find page of a Garmin GPS receiver, left, and list of geocaches on a Garmin touchscreen GPS, right. These GPS receivers feature paperless geocaching, which lets you upload complete information on a geocache to your GPS.

Special Geocaching GPS Features

Newer GPS receivers have several features to make geocaching easier. On these receivers, you can go directly to a list of geocaches on the GPS. For example, to find geocaches you've exported to a Garmin trail GPS receiver, press "FIND", and then select "Geocache". A geocache waypoint may have a special waypoint symbol to indicate that it's an unfound or found geocache. The latest GPS receivers feature "Paperless Geocaching", a feature allowing you to load all of the notes associated with the geocache into your receiver, avoiding the need to print and carry a paper copy of the description.

Placing A Geocache

When you decide to place a cache, you are taking on the responsibility to locate it carefully and legally as well as to maintain it.

Find a location

Choose the place for your cache carefully. Most geocachers place caches in places that mean something to them, such as along a favorite walk or hiking trail, in a park near their home or work, or near a place of historical significance.

- Make sure it meets the www.geocaching.com or www.opencaching.com requirements
- Place it where casual visitors won't find it, such as just off a road or trail and out of sight
- Get permission before placing a cache on private land
- Geocaches are not allowed in National Parks
- Don't place a cache where it could cause concern by being confused with something dangerous
- Do not place a cache near a nest or other critical wild animal activity

Prepare Your Cache

Cache Containers

Pack your cache in a small, waterproof container. A clean plastic food storage box works well, as does a plastic jar with a waterproof lid. You can buy special geocache containers, notebooks, and many other geocaching supplies and notebooks at shop.groundspeak.com, www.rei.com, and www.amazon.com. Be sure to label the outside of the container as a geocache and provide the name of the geocache as well as contact information.

Cache Contents

At a minimum, include a logbook and a pencil. Pens freeze and fail in locations that experience subfreezing temperatures. Include a note to explain the purpose of the cache. Optionally, you can include small items to be traded. Again, never place food in a cache.

 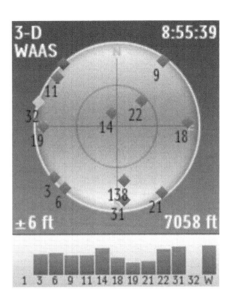

Left, position averaging on a Garmin trail GPS. Right, DeLorme trail GPS receiving WAAS corrections, improving accuracy to 6 feet.

Placing Your Cache

It is critical that you get accurate GPS coordinates for your new geocache. These coordinates are the heart of the sport. Turn on your GPS when you arrive at the site and leave it in a spot with a clear view of the sky while you prepare the cache. Although a GPS receiver can get a fix in as little as 15 seconds, the accuracy of the fix improves over time as it locks onto more satellites. You should let the receiver work for at least 15 minutes before marking the cache waypoint. If your GPS receiver has position averaging, use it. If your unit supports the Wide Area Augmentation System (WAAS), you should use it. Once you have the most accurate waypoint you can obtain, save it in the GPS receiver and mark it on the geocache container and in the logbook. As a backup, write down the coordinates in your field notebook or save them on your voice recorder.

Submitting Your Cache

Go to geocaching.com or opencaching.com and follow the instructions to submit your cache.

Before a cache will be accepted for listing, it will be reviewed by a volunteer to make sure it meets these guidelines. Because neither site verifies the physical location, the person placing the cache is responsible for its placement and care.

Maintaining Your Cache

After placing your cache, it is your responsibility to maintain it. Return to your geocache as often as necessary to make certain it hasn't been disturbed. If special circumstances arise (the geocache is buried under snow or the area is flooded), note that on your geocache's online listing.

Benchmarking

Benchmarking is a sub category of geocaching where you hunt for benchmarks instead of geocaches. Benchmarks are small metal disks or other permanent marks placed and recorded by government surveyors to precisely mark a location. They are placed for many different reasons, including map making, highway and bridge construction, general land surveys, and marking boundaries, among others. Many U.S. benchmarks are part of the National Spacial Reference System maintained by the National Geodetic Survey (NGS). You can find benchmarks near you by searching the benchmark database at www.geocaching.com/mark/. There are currently over 736,000 benchmarks in the database.

Benchmark placed by the U.S. Geologic Survey.

Benchmarks hide in plain sight and are generally ignored by the public, though some of them are of historic value. Many have not had an official visitor since first placed by the original surveyors. The database on geocaching.com is linked to the government database maintained by NGS. You can see the datasheet written by the original surveyors, updates from later official visits, and logs left by fellow amateur benchmarkers, and you can add your own comments and photos to the log.

Although a GPS receiver makes it easier to find the general location of a benchmark, to find the actual mark you will need to refer to the datasheet as well as comments logged by later visitors, if any. Most benchmarks were placed before GPS existed, so the description in the datasheet relies on landmarks to locate the benchmark. The GPS coordinates for most benchmarks were derived from survey data and may not be accurate.

Refer to www.geocaching.com/mark/ for much more information on benchmarking. You can also search the NGS database directly, though as an unofficial user you can't log anything there: www.ngs.noaa.gov/cgi-bin/datasheet.prl

Waymark at El Tovar Hotel, Grand Canyon, a national historic landmark

Waymarking

Waymarking consists of recording the coordinates of interesting places throughout the world and sharing that information with everyone via the Web. Unlike geocaching, nothing physical is left at waymarked sites. Instead, waymarks are uploaded to a Web site and assigned to departments and categories such as "History- World Heritage Sites". On www.waymarking.com, the most popular waymarking Web site, there are currently more than 384,000 waymarks in 1,038 categories. Waymarks consist of GPS coordinates, short and long descriptions, photos, and a log where later visitors can record their visits.

The Complete Navigator

This chapter presents information that you'll want to know as you develop your navigation skills. The complete navigator not only knows how to use all the capabilities of their GPS receiver, they also should be comfortable with traditional map and compass navigation as well as route finding skills. This chapter is not intended to be a reference on traditional map and compass techniques. For that, I recommend the classic book by Bjorn Kjellstrom, *Be Expert with Map and Compass*. Since this book focuses on working with GPS and digital maps, those who want to learn the older methods of working with GPS and paper maps should refer to my earlier GPS book, *Basic Essentials Using GPS*, published by The Globe Pequot Press.

There is also a section on working with some of the features and capabilities of GPS receivers that haven't been covered in the previous chapters. In some cases there's more detail on topics that were mentioned earlier.

Datums

A "geodetic reference datum", or usually just "datum", is a set of reference points that are used for surveying and to create accurate maps. Any map accurate enough to use for navigation should have the datum printed in the margin. There are many different datums in use worldwide (just look at the list on your GPS setup page), but there are just three that are commonly used in North America: North American Datum 1927 (NAD27), NAD83, and World Geodetic System 1984 (WGS84).

- NAD27: An older U.S. datum that is the basis for most USGS topographic maps.

- NAD83: A U.S. datum that is the basis for WGS84. Essentially the same as WGS84.

- WGS84: The datum used by GPS and most maps developed since GPS became operational. WGS84 is the only worldwide datum.

The reason that datum matters is that when working with either paper or digital maps, your GPS receiver must be set to the same datum used by the map, otherwise coordinates plotted on the map or transferred to the GPS receiver or computer will be in error. The error can be anything from a few feet to many miles, especially when working with maps produced outside of North America. GPS receivers always use WGS84 internally and convert coordinates to the selected datum for display.

Geographic Coordinate Systems

A geographic coordinate system is a set of numbers and letters used to describe a specific location on the Earth's surface as precisely as the user desires. There are many different coordinate systems in use (again, just look at the list on your GPS receiver's setup page), but only two are in common use for GPS navigation, latitude and longitude (lat/long) and Universal Transverse Mercator (UTM). Each has advantages and disadvantages for GPS navigation.

Latitude and Longitude

Lat/long is based on a global system of latitude, which is the distance north or south of the equator measured from 0 to 90 degrees, and longitude, which is the distance east or west of the Prime Meridian measured from 0 to 180 degrees. By international agreement, the Prime Meridian is located at the Royal Observatory in Greenwich, U.K. (near London.) Degrees are further broken down into minutes (1/60th of a degree) and seconds (1/60th of a minute.) One minute of latitude is approximately one nautical mile, or 1.15 statute (road) miles. Meridians are lines of constant longitude which converge at the poles. Because of this convergence, one minute of longitude is the same horizontal distance as a minute of latitude only at the equator. Parallels are lines of constant latitude, and they are parallel to each other and the equator. Lat/long may be expressed in degrees, minutes, and decimal seconds (DMS), degrees and decimal minutes, or decimal degrees. The choice of format depends on the application; all three forms may be used to specify a precise location and GPS receivers can be set to display any of these formats. As an example, DMS lat/long coordinates are written as N35° 24' 23" W136° 14' 45". Sometimes positive numbers are used to depict north latitude and east longitude, and negative for south latitude and west longitude. To avoid confusion, it is best to use the direction letters.

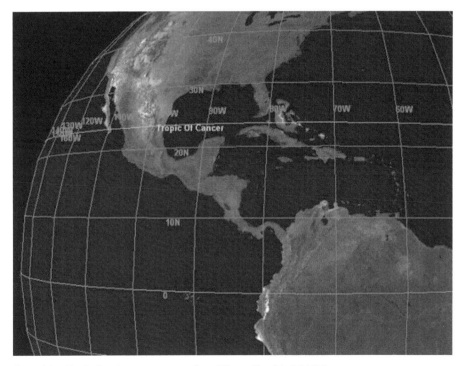

Part of the Earth showing convergence of meridians. Graphic: NASA

Advantages of Lat/Long

Lat/Long is found on all maps that are worthy of the name, including globes, atlases of all sorts, road maps, recreational maps, planimetric maps, and topographic maps, as well as on aeronautical and marine charts. If a map doesn't have lat/long or another coordinate system, use the map for informational purposes only and not for navigation. Lat/long is universally understood by cartographers and navigators and anyone concerned with precise location on the Earth's surface. Lat/long is preferred for long-distance navigation by ships and aircraft.

Disadvantages of Lat/Long

A practical difficulty in the field for the recreational user comes from the convergence of meridians. Look at a USGS topographic map for anywhere at middle latitudes and you can see that degrees of latitude and longitude are not equal. This makes it difficult to accurately plot lat/long on a topo without a special plotter.

Universal Transverse Mercator

UTM was developed by the U.S. Department of Defense to address the problem of convergence of meridians. The system is based on a square metric grid that breaks the Earth into 60 zones. These zones are six degrees of longitude wide and extend from the equator to 80 degrees south latitude and 84 degrees north latitude. A separate system, Universal Polar Stereographic (UPS), is used at the poles. Each zone is designated by a number starting from 180° west longitude and increasing to the east. Each zone is further broken down into zone letters, each letter representing eight degrees of latitude. Zone letters are not actually needed to describe a position, but they are usually displayed on your GPS receiver's position page. Within each numbered zone, positions are described by the number of meters east, or "easting", of a reference line that is always west of the zone boundary. This means the easting is always positive. The other coordinate, "northing", is the number of meters north of the equator (or north of the 80 degree south meridian in the southern hemisphere.) UTM coordinates describing a location to one meter accuracy look like this:

   Zone 12 441283mE 3897246mN

On a trail GPS receiver, the satellite page gives the same coordinates as:

   12 S 0441283 3897246 ("S" is the zone letter)

If one meter precision is not needed, the right-hand digits may be left off. The same coordinates accurate to 1000 meters, or one kilometer, would read:

   Zone 12 441mE 3897mN

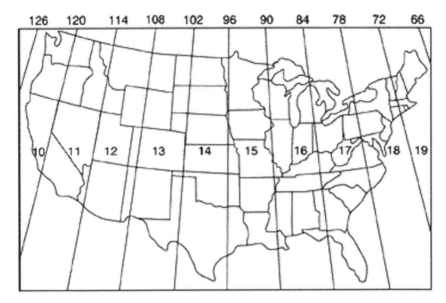

UTM zones covering the 48 contiguous states

Advantages of UTM

Again, the major advantage of UTM is that it uses a square metric grid so that there is no convergence of grid lines. In addition, only positive whole numbers are used to describe coordinates. Because of these two factors, UTM is much easier to use in the field than lat/long and has become the preferred coordinate system for search and rescue teams and many other field workers. All USGS topo maps, some privately produced maps, and nearly all digital maps have UTM coordinates. It is easy to plot UTM coordinates on a paper map without a special plotter.

Disdvantages of UTM

The only real problems with UTM are the fact that most people have never heard of it and that many paper maps don't have a UTM grid. Because we're working with digital maps and computer printouts which can display UTM coordinates, UTM is the coordinate system of choice in this book.

Other Navigational Units

Distance and Speed

While most of the world has gone metric, the United States is still burdened with the awkward English system. Land navigation in the U.S. uses statute miles for distance and speed measurements. As you approach a waypoint closely, you'll notice that your receiver displays feet instead of miles. Marine navigation uses nautical miles and knots (nautical miles per hour) and sea kayakers using marine charts will want to set those units on their GPS receivers. The rest of the world can just select "Metric" from the units page.

Elevation and Rate of Climb or Descent

Feet and feet per minute are used in the U.S., while the rest of the world uses meters and meters per second or meters per minute.

Barometric Pressure

You'll obtain the barometric pressure in one of three units in order to calibrate the altimeter on your GPS receiver. The U.S. public and international aviation both use inches of mercury (in. Hg), meteorologists use millibars in the U.S., and the rest of the world uses hectopascals.

Degrees

Often you don't have to know the actual bearing in degrees in order to navigate. But it helps to know that bearing, headings, and courses are measured in degrees, with north at 0 degrees, east at 90 degrees, south at 180 degrees, and west at 270 degrees.

Magnetic Variation

Magnetic compasses do not point to true north, the location of the geographic north pole. Instead, they point to the magnetic north pole which is in northeastern Canada about 1000 miles from the geographic north pole. The difference between true and magnetic north is the "variation". GPS receivers that have internal magnetic compasses automatically compensate for variation and use true north by default. If you're using a hand held compass without a variation (sometimes called "declination") adjustment, you will have to convert between true and magnetic bearings. As mentioned earlier, I strongly recommend that your hand held compass have declination adjustment to avoid confusion in the field.

Paper Chase

Just as the advent of personal computers has not resulted in the mythical "paperless office", computer-based, digital maps have not made paper maps obsolete. Paper maps are more useful than ever. With digital map programs, you can print topo maps customized for your outdoor adventure. You can show GPS routes and waypoints that you've planned in advance, as well as freehand routes and elevation profiles. You can print maps at any desired scale, and you can print UTM grids to make field plotting of waypoints much easier.

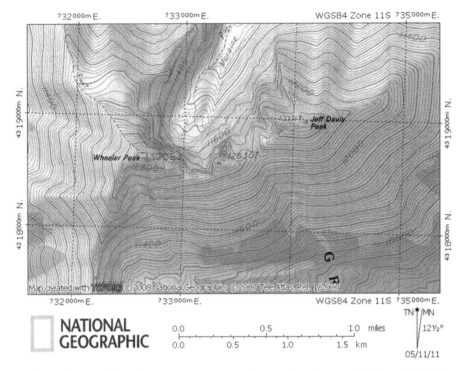

0.0		0.5		1.0	miles
0.0	0.5	1.0	1.5	km	

*Reading UTM coordinates from a paper map printed with a blue dashed UTM grid. TOPO!,
©2010 National Geographic*

Reading Coordinates

Occasionally, you'll need to read coordinates from a printed map. This commonly happens in the field when you decide to navigate to a place you've identified on your map. For example, let's say that you want the UTM coordinates for Jeff Davis Peak on the map above. First, note the datum, WGS84, and the UTM zone, 11, which are printed on the lower right margin. Find the easting by reading from the nearest UTM grid line (the fine dashed lines) to the west, in this case 734000. Using the kilometer scale (1 kilometer = 1000 meters) at the bottom of the map, you can estimate that Jeff Davis Peak is about 150 meters east of the grid line, which makes the easting 734150. The northing is easy because the peak is almost on the 4319000 grid line. Using the kilometer scale again, the estimated northing is 4318950. The complete UTM coordinates would read: Zone 11 734150mE 4318950mN. We've estimated a position within 50 meters (164 feet) using just the features of the map.

Plotting Coordinates

Sometimes you'll need to plot coordinates on a paper map. On the example map above, plot WGS84 Zone 11 732658mE 4318627mN. First, find the easting by going to the 732000 grid line. Then estimate 658 meters using the kilometer scale. Do the same with the northing, starting from the 4318000 grid line and estimating 627 meters north. That puts this UTM coordinate at Wheeler Peak.

Lost!

Every experienced outdoor person has been lost, or as Daniel Boone put it, "a mite confused." The key to not getting lost is simple- stay found. As you travel through the backcountry, whether on a trail or cross-country, keep track of your position. If you know the country well, you can just note familiar landmarks as you pass them. If the country is new, watch for distinctive landmarks, save waypoints, and make note of them on your map. If you're on a trail, don't entirely trust the trail signs. Signs can be wrong, moved, or totally missing. Also, look back the way you came. Landmarks look different from the opposite direction.

If you do lose the trail or become unsure of where you are, stop immediately, take a break and have some water and a snack. Pressing on in the face of confusion is a serious mistake and only makes the situation worse. You need to take time to think before doing anything. Once the first rush of panic is over, think about when you were last certain you were on the trail or correct route. Look at your GPS map page and note the last waypoint you passed. Then, backtrack carefully to that point. Once there, look carefully for the correct route. Don't continue until you are certain you're on the right route.

Another method of locating a lost trail is to walk in widening circles around your stopping point. Before starting the search, mark your stopping point as a waypoint in the GPS.

Even if your GPS fails and your map is destroyed in a rainstorm, you can always head for your baseline as long as you can determine the general direction to travel.

Cellular Phones and Rescue

Don't ever count on a cell phone for rescue from backcountry and wilderness areas. Even a satellite phone may not have a signal when you need it. Although coverage gets better all the time, the cell network is designed to serve cities, highways, towns, and rural areas, in that order. Towers are built where the most customers are.

Personal Locator Beacons

If you explore remote areas, consider carrying a Personal Locator Beacon. PLB's use the international Search and Rescue and GPS satellite systems and are registered to the owner. When you activate your PLB, the SAR center receives your precise location and contact information within minutes. ACR makes the lightweight ResqLink PLB which is ideal for the wilderness traveler: http://bit.ly/qtcvWh.

Essentials

Even after rescuers are alerted, you have to stay alive until they reach you, which will be hours or days. Always be prepared for changing weather, slow members of your party, and injuries. On all but the shortest treks, carry the essential basic gear.

- Water
- Extra food
- Extra clothing
- Rain gear
- Map
- Compass
- Knife
- Lighter or fire starter
- Flashlight or headlamp
- First aid kit
- Space blanket or other emergency shelter

For more information on backcountry emergencies, especially in desert regions, see my book, *Desert Sense: Camping, Hiking & Biking in Hot, Dry Climates*, published by Mountaineers Books and available on the Kindle and in paperback.

Waypoints

Waypoints are the heart of GPS navigation and there's much more you can do with them than has been covered in the examples so far.

Man Overboard Waypoints

MOB waypoints are special waypoints available in all marine GPS units and some trail GPS receivers. The MOB feature lets you instantly mark a position and start navigating toward it. On a GPS with the MOB feature, press and hold the "MOB" button until the MOB message pops up asking if you wish to save a MOB waypoint and start navigating toward it. Press "ENTER" to do so. MOB waypoints are mainly useful on the water for power boaters and sailors.

Finding Waypoints Page

The find waypoints page on a trail GPS receiver lets you search for waypoints by name, symbol, or in order of the nearest waypoints. You can also search for recently found waypoints. Depending on the mapping data that is installed on, or you've added to, your GPS, you can also search for cities, freeway exits, and other points of interest.

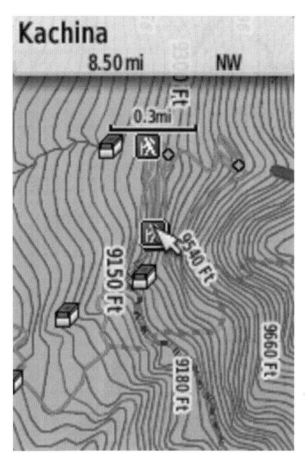

Map page with panned pointer on a Garmin trail GPS. You can navigate directly to any point on the map by pointing to it and then pressing ENTER to create a waypoint.

Creating Waypoints with the Map Page

If you have detailed maps on your GPS, you can navigate to a distant landmark by locating it on the GPS map and creating a waypoint there. To do this on a trail GPS unit, go to the map page and pan the map to the distant landmark. Zoom in as necessary to see the exact location you desire, then stop moving the pointer. If the pointer is near a known landmark on the map, a label pops up. If there is more than one landmark near the pointer, a list pops up. Select the desired landmark. The waypoint page appears with the waypoint already named to the landmark name, You can save it as a waypoint or select "Go To" to immediately start navigating toward it. If there is no landmark near the cursor, you'll be asked if you want to create a user waypoint there.

Projected Waypoint

003

250 degrees
4.00 miles

Save

Save and Edit

Waypoint page on a Garmin trail GPS for a new waypoint projected 250 degrees and 4.0 miles from the starting waypoint

Projecting with Bearing and Distance

You can use an existing waypoint to project a new waypoint if you know its bearing and distance from the existing waypoint. First, find the existing waypoint and select it to bring up the waypoint page. Then, on a trail GPS receiver, press "MENU" and select "Project Waypoint". The GPS unit creates a new waypoint. At the bottom of the waypoint page, enter the bearing and distance of the new waypoint, then select "Go To" to start navigation.

Proximity Waypoints

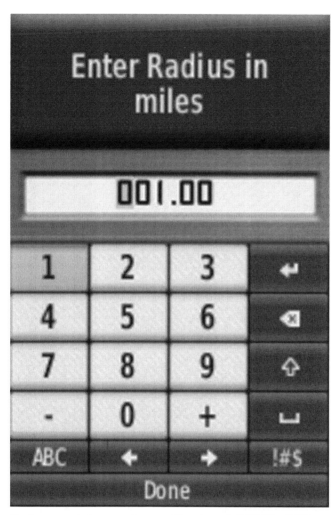

Setting a proximity waypoint on a Garmin trail GPS. The GPS receiver will now warn if you approach within 1.0 mile of the selected waypoint.

A proximity waypoint lets you define an alarm radius around a waypoint. When you approach closer than the selected distance, the GPS receiver sounds an alarm. To set a proximity waypoint on GPS receivers with this feature, go to the main menu and select "Proximity", then select the desired waypoint and set the radius for the proximity warning.

Sun and Moon Data

Sun and moon data for a waypoint on a Garmin trail GPS

Sunrise and sunset data is extremely useful in the backcountry for planning your day to take advantage of available daylight. Knowing the time of sunset lets you know when to start looking for a campsite or when you should return to your vehicle to avoid being caught out in the dark.

To view sun and moon data on a Garmin trail GPS for your current location, go to the main menu and select "Sun and Moon". The sun and moon page shows sunrise and sunset, moonrise and moonset, moon phase, and position of the sun and moon in the sky for the selected waypoint at the current time. You can change the date, time, and location.

Hunt and Fish

Hunt and fish data for a waypoint on a Garmin trail GPS

To view hunt and fish data on a Garmin trail GPS for your current location, go to the main menu and select "Hunt and Fish". The hunt and fish page makes an overall prediction and shows the best times and good times for the selected waypoint at the current time. You can change the date and time as well as the location from this page.

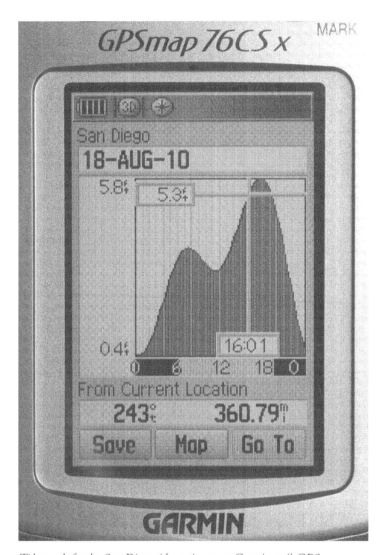

Tide graph for the San Diego tide station on a Garmin trail GPS

Sea kayakers and coastal boaters need tide information to plan paddles to take advantage of tidal currents, and also to avoid hazardous tidal rips. Coastal hikers can use the tide data to avoid being trapped against seacoast cliffs by a rising tide.

To view tidal information at a tide station on a Garmin trail GPS, select Tides from the main menu. Select a tide station and press "ENTER". The tide page shows a graph of the tide for the current day.

Using Tracks

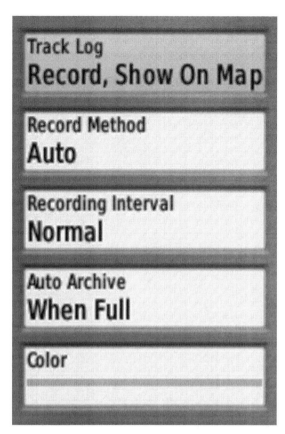

Track setup page on a Garmin trail GPS

As mentioned earlier, tracks are waypoints saved automatically by the GPS receiver as you travel, unless you disable track logging. Although you can't work with track waypoints directly, you can change how tracks are recorded, turn the track log on and off, and save all or part of a track log to internal memory or a memory card.

Track Setup

The track setup page on most trail GPS units lets you turn the track log on and off, and shows how much internal memory is used by the track log. You can also save or clear the track log and start backtrack navigation to retrace your route. Select "Setup" to see the track setup page. Here you have the option to have the track log wrap when full, that is, overwrite old data with new. You can set the record method to Auto, Time, or Distance. If Method is set to Auto, then Interval gives you a range of five intervals. If Method is set to Time, then Interval lets you specify the time, and if Method is set to Distance, then you can specify the distance interval at which track points are recorded. For most uses, Auto works well. An exception is measuring trail distance at walking speeds. As mentioned earlier, the error on Auto is about 5% due to GPS position errors. Accuracy can be increased by setting the track interval to 30 seconds.

The track setup page also lets you change the color of displayed tracks on the map, and also save tracks to a micro SD card.

Saving Tracks

When you save a track, you're given the option of saving the entire track log or a portion of it. If you opt to save a portion, the map page appears and you can scroll the pointer to select the beginning and the end of the portion you wish to save. Saved tracks are automatically named with the date and a number, if more than one track is saved on the same date. You can rename them to a meaningful name, such as "Camp to Car".

The latest GPS receivers let you navigate along any saved track in either direction. When you select a track to navigate, the GPS receiver creates a route along the track, including any waypoints you've saved along the track. You can navigate with both the map and compass pages, as needed.

Profiling Saved Tracks

You can also create an elevation profile for a saved track by selecting the track and pressing "MENU."

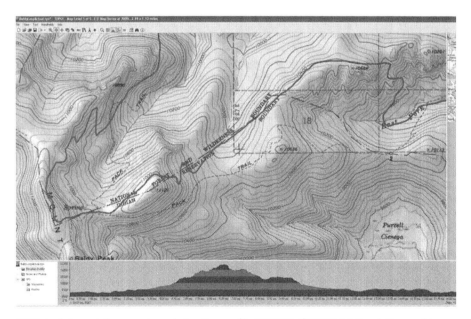

GPS track imported as a route and elevation profile. TOPO!, ©2010 National Geographic

Measuring Trail Distance with Tracks

As explained earlier in the book, a GPS receiver should not be used to measure trail distances at walking speeds. But there is a simple way to use recorded GPS track data to measure trail distance. Just import the GPS data into a digital map program. For example, using National Geographic Topo!, import the track as a freehand route. Don't import as waypoints because the program will generate far too many. Then right-click on the track using the Route tool and create an elevation profile. With the profile, you can measure the length of the entire trail as well as segments of the trail. You can also see the total elevation change and the amount of change along any segment.

Working with Routes

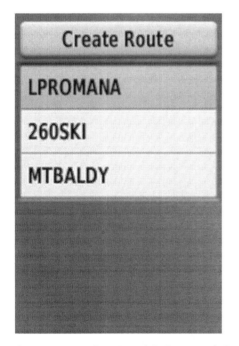

Route pages on Garmin and DeLorme trail GPS receivers showing the saved routes

A GPS route is a collection of saved waypoints describing the route to get from a starting waypoint to an ending waypoint. To activate an exiting route or create a new route, select the Routes page from the main menu of your GPS receiver. You can rename the routes and edit the waypoints in the route.

Editing Waypoints in a Route

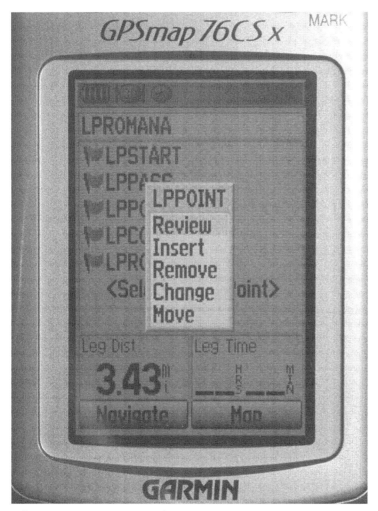

Editing a route on a Garmin trail GPS

To edit a waypoint in a route, select the route and then the waypoint you wish to edit. A menu lets you review, insert, remove, change, or move a waypoint. If the route is active, changes affect both the active route and the saved route.

Starting and Stopping Navigation

To start navigation on a route on a trail GPS, select Where To from the main menu or press the Find button. Then select the desired route. To stop navigation, select Where To from the main menu or press the Find button, then select Stop Navigation.

Map Page

The map page is probably the one you'll use most often for navigation, and it has many settings that allow you to customize it for your needs. Press "MENU" while on the map page of most trail GPS receivers to get a list of map page options. You can stop navigation, recalculate the route (used for street navigation), decide when guidance text is shown, set up the map page, measure distance on the map, and declutter the map.

Measuring Distance

To measure distance from your present position on the map page of most trail GPS receivers, press "MENU" and select "Measure Distance". Using the four-way controller, move the pointer to the desired point. The sceen will show the distance and bearing from the starting point as you move the pointer.

Map Setup Options

To reach the map setup page on most trail GPS units, go to the map page, press "MENU", and then select "Setup." You can also reach map setup from the "Setup" menu item. There are many map options that can be set and it takes many pages to show them all. Most of the options set the amount of detail shown on the map at various zoom levels.

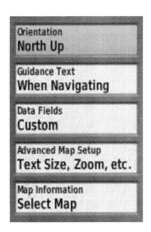

Map setup pages on a Garmin trail GPS, left, and Delorme trail GPS, right

If you're a boater, you'll probably change map orientation to "Track Up" when you are traveling in straight route segments, such as when paddling on open water. This changes the map orientation as you travel and always keeps your current direction of travel toward the top of the map. A small pointer constantly points north as your direction of travel changes. North Up map orientation is better for travel on land because it keeps the map in a constant orientation as you follow the twists and turns of a road or trail.

Compass Page

There are a couple of options on the compass page that you may want to change depending on your mode of travel. You can do this by pressing "MENU" while on the compass page of most trail GPS receivers.

Bearing and Course Pointers

The bearing pointer always shows the direction, or bearing, to the next waypoint. You'll probably prefer the bearing pointer when you are following a trail or road or walking cross-country across all but the most open terrain. The bearing pointer always shows you which way to turn to keep traveling toward your destination.

The course pointer points toward the next waypoint and an offset segment shows how far off course you are and which way to turn to get back on course. It is most useful when traveling straight route segments, such as sailing across open water.

Sight and Go Navigation

Sight and Go on newer Garmin trail GPS receivers lets you use the GPS compass page to walk a bearing line toward a distant landmark in the same way you'd use a mechanical compass. To use Sight and Go from the compass page on a Garmin GPS receiver, press "MENU", then select "Sight 'N Go". Use the sighting mark and the course arrow to point the GPS receiver toward the desired landmark. Remember to hold the GPS receiver level, unless your receiver has a 3-axis compass. Select "Lock Course" and then "Set Course". If you wish, you can project a waypoint on the locked bearing by entering an estimated distance, then use "Go To" navigation to navigate toward the projected waypoint.

Compass setup pages on a Garmin trail GPS, left, and a DeLorme trail GPS, right

Altimeter Page

The altimeter page is used for viewing elevation profiles of your route or track and also for showing changes in barometric pressure over time.

Time and Distance Elevation Plots

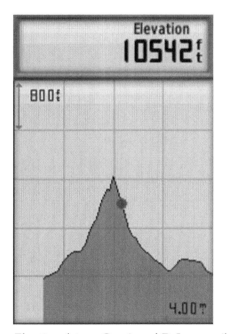 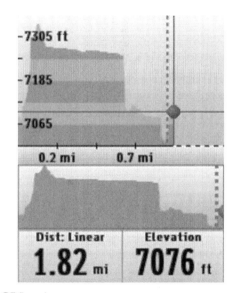

Elevation plots on Garmin and DeLorme trail GPS receivers

Elevation plots of your track or route are most useful when shown over distance. You can plot the elevation graph for a route before you travel it to get a picture of the elevation change. Elevation plots are available from the main menu of most trail GPS receivers. You can zoom in and out and move the cursor to view details of the profile.

Pressure Plots

Pressure plots can show sea-level-corrected barometer readings or the ambient pressure. Sea-level-corrected readings are useful if you've been stopped for a while, such as at camp on a multi-day trip. Trends in the barometer are an important clue to changes in the weather. For example, a steadily falling barometer usually means bad weather is approaching.

Customizing Your GPS Pages

The data fields on the main pages of most trail GPS receivers can be customized to show the data you select. Some newer GPS receivers come with preset profiles for activities such as hiking, hunting, boating, and geocaching. When an activity is selected, the GPS receiver settings are optimized for that activity. Any changes you make to settings are saved for that activity. You can also create and name custom activities. Saved activities are a great timesaver if you often change activities. While there is an infinite number of combinations of settings, here are a few suggestions for different outdoor activities:

Trail Hiking

- Trip Computer: Speed instead of Odometer at the bottom of the screen
- Map: No data fields, guidance text on while navigating (default)
- Active Route: Default
- Compass: Bearing pointer (default)
- Altimeter: Default

Cross-Country Hiking or Hunting

- Trip Computer: Speed instead of Odometer at the bottom of the screen
- Map: Default
- Active Route: Default
- Compass: Bearing pointer
- Altimeter: Default

Paddling

- Trip Computer: Big numbers, showing off course, time to next, and time to destination
- Map: Track up
- Active Route: Default
- Compass: Course pointer
- Altimeter: Default

Geocaching and Benchmarking

- Trip Computer: Default
- Map: Default
- Active Route: Default
- Compass: Bearing pointer (default)
- Altimeter: Default

Differential GPS

Differential GPS (DGPS) uses one or more ground-based reference systems to transmit correction information to GPS receivers to compensate for atmospheric and other errors. A reference station is set up on a known surveyed point. The reference station receives the GPS signals, computes the difference between the GPS position and its known position, and transmits the correction to GPS receivers in the area that are equipped with a special DGPS receiver. Accuracy of less than three meters can be achieved.

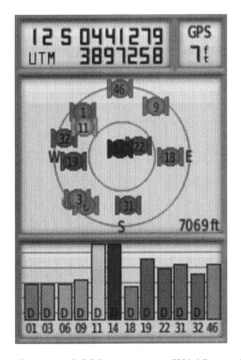
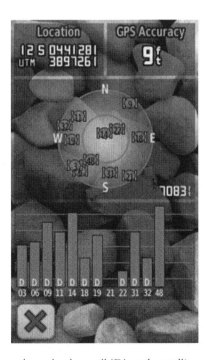

Garmin trail GPS units receiving WAAS corrections, as shown by the small 'D' on the satellite signal strength bars. Accuracy is 7 and 9 feet

There are several different types of DGPS. Coastal systems are set up by the U.S. and Canadian Coast Guards to increase the accuracy of ship navigation in shipping lanes and harbors. Government agencies and surveyors set up DGPS stations in their areas of responsibility or at a construction site. The U.S. Federal Aviation Administration runs a satellite-based DGPS system, the Wide Area Augmentation System (WAAS), which increases the accuracy of GPS to less than three meters so that it can be used for aircraft instrument approaches to airports in bad weather. Most trail GPS receivers can use WAAS, but not under all conditions. Since the WAAS signals are transmitted from geostationary satellites 22,000 miles above the Earth you may not be able to receive WAAS corrections when the sky is partially obscured by trees or canyon walls. On a Garmin trail GPS, WAAS reception is shown by small letter "D"s in each satellite's signal strength bar on the satellite status page. On DeLorme trail GPS units, WAAS reception is shown by green signal strength bars.

Pitfalls

As wonderful as GPS is, it is not perfect. Like any tool, it has limitations, and you need to understand them to avoid being caught by surprise. And since GPS receivers can and will fail, a competent outdoor person also knows traditional map and compass navigation, as discussed in the previous chapter.

No Power, No Fix

It may seem obvious, but when the batteries in your GPS receiver run down, the unit stops working! Even so, it's amazing how few people carry spare batteries for their GPS. And of course, it's always possible to drop the GPS receiver and break it.

Datum Doldrums

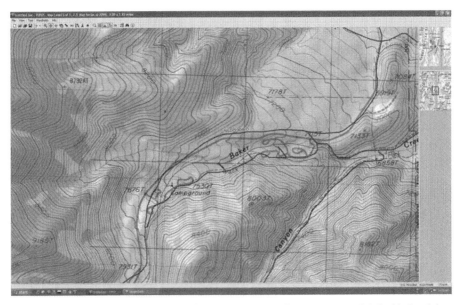

Datum error on a topo map displayed in Topo! with two different UTM grids. The black solid UTM grid is based on NAD27, and the blue dashed UTM grid is based on WGS84. TOPO!, ©2010 National Geographic

As mentioned earlier, setting the wrong datum into a GPS receiver can result in large position errors when working with paper and digital maps. The map above is displayed with two UTM grids in one kilometer squares. The black solid lines are based on the NAD27 datum, and the blue dashed lines are based on WGS84. You can see the position error between the two grids.

Check the map margin for the datum. If it's not there, use WGS84. Changing the datum changes the values displayed for the coordinates on the GPS screen, not the actual position of the waypoint. So if you're navigating with a GPS receiver and its internal maps alone, without reference to paper maps, then the datum doesn't matter. But you may end up working with paper maps anyway.

Here's a possible scenario: You're hiking cross-country with some friends in an area you know well, so although you have a GPS receiver, a printed map, and compass as backups, you don't need any of them. That is, until a member of the party slips on a rock and breaks their ankle. After realizing there's no way your small group can evacuate the victim, you call for a rescue on your cell phone. The dispatcher asks for your location and you describe it as well as you can with landmarks. She then asks if you have a GPS. The rescue team leader takes the coordinates from your GPS, which is set to WGS84, and plots them on a USGS topo map, which uses NAD27. The result is that the rescue helicopter doesn't find you at the location the crew expected and has to fly a search pattern, wasting time and money.

No Satellites

Although the current batch of GPS units with high-sensitivity receivers is far better at getting a fix with a partial view of the sky than older units, there are still limits. If the receiver can see the entire, unobstructed sky, it will always get a 4-satellite fix (unless it's being jammed, but that won't happen for ground users unless they are near a military base that is testing a GPS jamming system.) However, if the sky is partially obscured by obstacles such as high canyon walls or dense forest canopy, the receiver may not be able to lock on to enough satellites for a 4-satellite fix. The GPS signals from the satellites are very weak and travel line-of-sight. In slot canyons in places such as the American Southwest, there may not be enough sky for the GPS to get a fix at all.

In heavy forest, the GPS receiver may not be able to maintain a 4-satellite fix while you are moving, but might if you stop and stay in one place for a few minutes. In this case it's better to save batteries by leaving the GPS off and only turning it on to get a position fix when you're stopped for a break.

When GPS is Useless

The GPS receiver doesn't know about the terrain that may lie between waypoints. The classic example is the motorist that tried to drive across a washed-out highway bridge because the street GPS told him to. In some areas, such as the Grand Canyon, relying on GPS navigation will get you into trouble in a hurry. Because the Grand Canyon has some of the most complex terrain in the world, routes are never in a straight line, even for short distances. Instead, they follow sloping terraces between sheer cliffs, and constantly snake in and out of drainages and side canyons. Any attempt to walk directly to a critical landmark, such as a spring, will almost certainly bring you up against a sheer cliff or impossible side canyon. The result is the same whether you're navigating by GPS or by compass. In the Grand Canyon, you must know how to navigate by landmarks and the characteristics of the major rock formations. Only in rare cases will a GPS receiver be useful to find an obscure landmark.

What to Buy

GPS Receivers

This chapter lists what to look for in a GPS receiver for outdoor use with digital maps and satellite imagery. This is not a buying guide, as no book can keep up with the rapid pace of new product and software introduction. It also doesn't cover features that don't have direct navigation uses, such as cameras, image viewers, audio players, and games. The best source for current product information is the company Web site. Most of the GPS manufacturers let you compare their various units, and also let you download the owners manuals before you buy. The chapter includes a list of company Web sites.

As mentioned in the Introduction, I strongly recommend that you buy a unit that has been on the market for a year or more. This gives the manufacturer time to discover and correct defects in the firmware that runs the receiver. The firmware on most GPS units can be upgraded by the user.

This book's companion Web site, www.ExploringGPS.com, recommends specific basic and advanced trail and street GPS receivers. In addition, a glossary explains GPS features and terminology, and there are links to the GPS manufacturers and sites with more information on GPS. For detailed reviews and comparison tables of trail and street GPS receivers, I suggest www.gpstracklog.com.

Civilian GPS receivers (as opposed to military) come in several different types:

- Street: These come with detailed street and road maps preloaded for specific areas. Different areas can usually be added later. Street GPS units are intended for highway and urban navigation by vehicle, and for urban navigation on foot. Street GPS receivers always have a touch-screen interface. They can be very useful for finding trailheads, boat ramps, and other jumping-off points for outdoor recreationists, especially in developed or well-established recreation areas. Often, back roads, trailheads, and public campgrounds are not shown.

- Trail: Hand-held receivers optimized for travel on foot, horseback, paddle craft, bicycle, and for use on trails, water, and in backcountry navigation. Trail units are either basic, or mapping:

Basic: No base map, or a very general base map. Maps cannot be added.

Mapping: Detailed base maps are built-in, and detailed topographic, marine charts, and street mapping may be preloaded and can always be added later. A mapping GPS receiver is a must for backcountry use with digital maps. Can be used for road navigation, but not as good for this purpose as a street GPS. Most mapping GPS receivers can also use marine charts, which are useful for sea kayakers and other paddlers navigating along coastal waters or large inland lakes and rivers.

- Marine: Designed for permanent mounting on power boats and sailboats. They are often combined with fish-finders. Their use is beyond the scope of this book.

- Aviation: Hand-held or permanently-mounted units with air navigation databases. Their use is beyond the scope of this book.

- Surveying and Scientific: Designed for precision surveying, scientific, and engineering work. These applications are also beyond the scope of this book.

Buying a Trail GPS

While all civilian GPS units have the same accuracy, there are many other differences, and the specifications can be confusing. This list shows what to look for in advanced trail GPS units for use with digital maps and trip-sharing Web sites.

- Display: Color screens are best for displaying topo maps and are more readable in sunlight.

- Batteries: Most receivers use two or three AA batteries. The unit should be able to use both NiMH rechargeable and lithium single-use batteries. Lithium batteries have the longest life under outdoor conditions, but NiMH batteries can be recharged hundreds of times. Get the newer NiMH batteries that retain their charge during storage. On day trips, my preference is to use NiMH batteries and carry lithium batteries as a backup. For backpack trips, I use lithium batteries exclusively, keeping one set in the receiver and one or more sets as spares, depending on the length of the trip.

- Battery Life: The receiver should run for least 12 hours continuously. Batteries will last many days if the unit is turned on only for position checks. Look for a receiver with a "Battery Saver" setting.

- Waterproof: Essential for outdoor use, but don't count on the waterproofing to hold up under heavy rain or continuous submersion in salt water.

- Floats: A good feature for boaters.

- High-sensitivity Receiver: These work much better in forest and areas such as canyons with a restricted view of the sky.

- WAAS: The Wide Area Augmentation System uses ground stations and satellites to increase accuracy to three meters or better. Most current trail GPS receivers can optionally use WAAS, a feature geocachers and benchmarkers should look for.

- Interface: USB is now the standard. High speed USB is desirable if you plan to upload large amounts of map data to your GPS receiver and for map updates. The USB port is also used to run the GPS receiver from external power.

- Detailed Base Map: Essential.

- Preloaded Maps: If you don't want to mess with loading maps on the GPS yourself, you can buy units with maps preloaded. On the other hand, there are many sources of free maps.

- Add-on Maps: You must be able to add maps after purchase.

- Routable Trails: Allows you to create routes that follow trails shown on the receiver's maps.

- Custom Maps: Allows you to load custom maps, including scanned paper maps. There are many free maps available on the Web.

- External Memory: The unit should accept micro-SD or SDHC memory cards, which are used for storing expanded map coverage as well as GPS data.

- Waypoint Memory: All mapping units have plenty of memory for waypoints.

- Geocaching: Special icons for found and unfound geocaches.

- Paperless Geocaching: Allows you to download complete geocaching data pages for use in the field.

- Profiles: Allows you to save customized settings for different activities.

- Route Memory: At least 50 saved routes.

- Track Log Memory: At least 20 saved tracks. Some units let you save tracks to micro-SD or SDHC cards.

- Automatic Routing: Turn-by-turn routing on roads- requires street mapping and trail units have small screens and no voice prompts.

- Touch screen: Not recommended for trail use because they are awkward to use in cold weather and with gloves. And buttons can be used without obscuring the screen or smearing it with dirt, sunscreen, and insect repellent.

- Electronic Compass: Lets you determine directions while not moving, just like a hand held compass. Newer GPS receivers have 3-axis electronic compasses that work when tilted, a feature not available in hand held compasses. You should always have a reliable liquid-filled, hand held compass as a backup.

- Barometric Altimeter: GPS-derived elevation is accurate to about 15 meters (49 feet) under ideal conditions. Since these conditions are often not met in the field, a calibrated barometric altimeter is more accurate. Some newer GPS receivers have an auto-calibrate setting for the altimeter, which uses GPS altitudes averaged over time to calibrate the barometric altimeter.

- Hunt/Fish Calendar: Yes, if you hunt or fish.

- Tide Tables: You'll need tidal information if you are a coastal boater or hiker.

- External Antenna Connector: If you plan to use your trail GPS extensively inside a vehicle, you may want to mount an external antenna on the roof of the vehicle.

Buying a Street GPS

Street units fall into three categories: Automotive, motorcycle, and trucking. Motorcycle units are waterproofed for exposure to weather and have features such as Bluetooth that allow riders to hear GPS spoken directions through helmet earphones. Trucker GPS receivers have routing optimized for truck routes. The following is a list of automotive street GPS features that are useful for navigating to trailheads, campgrounds, picnic areas, and such for outdoor users.

- Display: All street GPS units have color screens that are designed for use in bright light.

- Batteries: Internal, rechargeable lithium-ion batteries are standard. You'll use battery power mainly for trip planning before a trip. On the road, the unit should be powered from the vehicle for maximum screen brightness.

- Battery Life: Typically 3 to 4 hours, which is mainly a concern for bicyclists. Again, motorcycle riders and motorists should power the GPS from the vehicle.

- Powered Mount: The power/USB cable goes to the mount instead of the GPS receiver, so you don't have to connect the cable every time you mount the GPS unit.

- Waterproof: Essential for bicyclists and motorcyclists.

- High-sensitivity Receiver: All but the cheapest street GPS units have high-sensitivity receivers which work better in city high-rise areas and dense forest than older receivers.

- Interface: The receiver should use high-speed USB, which is used to update maps and upload new maps. The USB port is also used to run the GPS receiver from external power and charge its internal battery.

- Base Map: Yes.

- Preloaded Street Maps: Choose the area of coverage you use most.

- Add-on Maps: If you travel to regions not covered by the preloaded maps, you'll need to be able to buy and upload new coverage.

- External Memory: Unit should accept micro-SD or SDHC memory cards for additional map coverage.

- Waypoint/Favorites Memory: All street units have plenty of memory for waypoints, or "Favorites".

- Route Memory: Ten or more if you frequently travel specific, customized routes with multiple via points.

- Touch screen: Standard because it works well in a vehicle, although virtual keyboards are slow for entering names and addresses.

- Voice Prompts: Standard.

- Speaks Street Names: Much safer for drivers than looking at the screen for street names.

- Auto Re-route for Detours: The GPS calculates detours around accidents and construction sites.

- Route Setup: This lets you choose between fastest time, shortest distance, and off-road (direct) navigation.

- Route Avoidance: Very useful for avoiding toll roads, dirt roads, U-turns, etc.

- FM Traffic Data: Handy in major cities. Lifetime free traffic service comes with some units, while others charge a monthly subscription fee. The traffic service often doesn't work in rural areas.

- Speed Limits: Shows speed limits along major roads. Temporary speed limit changes, such as in construction zones, may not be shown.

- Emergency Location: This useful feature finds nearest hospitals, police stations, and gas stations, and shows the nearest address and intersection.

- Environment-Friendly Routing: Displays the most fuel-efficient route.

- Custom Points of Interest: Useful for saving frequent destinations as a "Favorite".

- External Antenna Connector: High-sensitivity receivers have pretty much eliminated the need for an external antenna. Note that street GPS receivers have the best view of the sky if mounted on the windshield, but windshield mounting is not legal in California and some other states. Most units work fine mounted on the dash.

GPS Receiver and Accessory Manufacturers

- DeLorme (www.delorme.com) makes the PN series of trail GPS receivers, a line of mapping software, and as GPS receiver modules for use with portable computers.

- Garmin (www.garmin.com) manufactures street, trail, marine, and aviation GPS receivers and mapping software.

- Lowrance (www.lowrance.com) manufactures mapping-type trail GPS receivers as well as marine GPS. The company also makes mapping software for use with its GPS units.

- Magellan (www.magellangps.com) makes GPS receivers as well as mapping software.

- RAM (www.ram-mount.com) makes a wide variety of vehicle, boat, and aircraft mounting systems for GPS and other electronic devices.

- Tom Tom (www.TomTom.com) makes street GPS units as well as bicycle GPS receivers.

- Trimble (www.trimble.com) produces GPS receivers and accessories for surveying, scientic, engineering, and other professional users.

Smart Phone or Dedicated GPS Receiver?

All cellular phones have GPS receivers built-in so that 911 services can locate callers. With the advent of smart phones, which are really pocket computers, a large and growing number of GPS applications or "apps" have appeared. There are several reasons why cell phone GPS should not be used in the backcountry:

- Cell phone GPS is designed for use in urban areas, not wilderness

- Battery life is short and batteries are proprietary

- Navigation and mapping apps may depend on having a data signal

- Software is designed for civilian use and is often buggy

Trail GPS receivers have serious advantages for backcountry use:

- Trail GPS antennas and receivers are much more sensitive

- Battery life is long and batteries are standard AAA or AA types that are field-replaceable

- Trail GPS software and hardware is often based on military and engineering designs and is more reliable

- Mapping and applications are stored internally and are not dependent on data signals

- Cost- a high-end mapping GPS with built in and free topo maps of the country can be bought for less than $350 and there are no monthly charges

At this stage of development, I strongly recommend that you get a trail GPS receiver for backcountry use rather than a smart phone. However, for front country, urban, and other non-critical use, cell phone apps are fun to play with.

Smart Phone Apps

Check online for the latest apps for your device:

- www.apple.com/iphone/apps-for-iphone
- na.blackberry.com/eng/services/appworld
- www.palm.com/us/products/software/mobile-applications.html
- www.nokiausa.com/ovi-services-and-apps
- www.microsoft.com/windowsmobile/en-us/downloads/default.mspx
- www.backpacker.com
- www.google.com/mobile/maps

Maps and Satellite Imagery

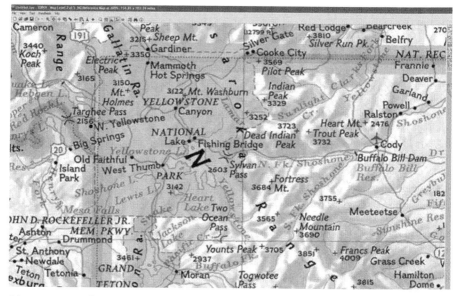

Planimetric map from TOPO!, ©2010 National Geographic

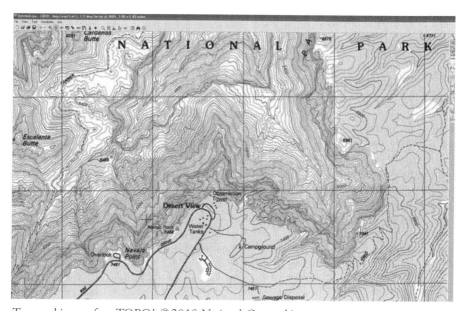

Topographic map from TOPO!, ©2010 National Geographic

Maps fall into two broad types, planimetric and topographic. Planimetric maps show mostly man-made features such as roads, trails, and buildings. Natural features such as rivers and mountain peaks may be shown, but the natural features are secondary to the man-made features. A highway or street map is a typical planimetric map. Topographic maps (commonly called topo maps) depict the shape of the land with contour lines, which are simply lines connecting points of equal elevation. Every fourth or fifth contour line is thicker. This simple device lets the map show landforms very well. Topo maps are by far the best maps for backcountry and wilderness travel, even if you stick to trails. With a topo, you can see how steeply a trail climbs or descends, find level areas for campsites, find water and fishing spots, determine if a stretch of country is forested, brushy, or open, and far more.

Paper Maps

As discussed in the The Complete Navigator chapter, paper maps are still important. Although the topo maps produced by the U.S. Geological Survey (and equivalent agencies in other countries) are the standard base maps for the country, they are not updated very often. Other agencies, such as the U.S. Forest Service, produce recreation maps of national forests and wilderness areas, with road, trail, and recreational information that is more up to date. These maps are very useful as supplements to printouts of digital maps.

U.S. Geologic Survey

You can buy printed copies and download free copies of government topo maps for the entire United States from USGS online at http://store.usgs.gov/. Historical maps are available from http://nationalmap.gov/historical.

Digital Maps

Offline maps can be used anytime you have your computer, since they are on CD, DVD, or loaded onto your hard drive. Online maps can only be used when you have a high-speed Internet connection.

Raster and Vector Maps

Digital maps for use on computers, GPS receivers, and smart phones are one of two types, raster and vector. Raster maps are scanned from paper maps, usually USGSS topo maps, and the scans vary in detail and quality. Since the base maps are not updated very often, man-made features tend to be out of date but the topography is very accurate.

Vector maps are generated from digital map data for display on the screen or for printing. These maps are usually more up to date for man-made features than raster maps, but don't show as much topographic detail.

GPSFileDepot

www.gpsfiledepot.com is one of the best Web sites for free maps and tutorials for GPS receivers.

DeLorme

DeLorme (www.delorme.com) produces Topo North America, a vector map product covering the U.S., Canada, and Mexico on DVD. Topo North America is an economical way to get wide area topographic map coverage. Topo North America is especially good for detailed street and road coverage. The topographic information isn't as detailed as USGS or National Geographic Topo! maps, but the road information is more up to date. You can download USGS topo maps, which DeLorme calls 3D TopoQuads, at extra cost. A variety of tools let you mark waypoints, draw routes and elevation profiles, draw shapes, add notes, and measure distance and area. You can also view maps in 3D. And you can share Topo North America route and GPS data online. Topo North America works with most GPS receivers, and DeLorme makes the Earthmate series of GPS receivers which are specifically designed for use with Topo North America.

EasyGPS

EasyGPS (www.easygps.com) is a free GPS mapping program. It is a simple way to transfer GPS data between your GPS receiver and your computer. It is also a good tool for archiving your GPS data in standard GPX format. Although EasyGPS maps your GPS data on screen, it does not use topo or planimetric maps.

Expert GPS

Expert GPS (www.expertgps.com) uses online USGS topo maps and aerial imagery as base maps. You can import and export GPS data in GPX and a wide variety of other formats. Tools let you draw routes, add symbols, and add text notes to the maps. A 30-day free trial is available.

Fugawi

Fugawi (www.fugawi.com) is designed primarily for use with their digital map products, which include marine charts as well as topo map coverage of much of the world. You can download maps to your hard drive for use offline.

Garmin Topo Maps and Satellite imagery

Available from www.garmin.com, Topo US 100K covers the entire US. Topo US 24K is available in regional sets. Both are vector maps designed for use with Garmin software and their mapping GPS receivers. Garmin also sells Birdseye satellite imagery for use with their GPS receivers and computer software.

Magellan

The company (www.magellangps.com) sells topo maps for use with their GPS receivers. Coverage includes the U.S., Canada, Mexico, and part of Europe.

Maptech

Maptech (www.MapTech.com) makes software with topo map coverage of the U.S. on CD and DVD. The program has tools for drawing routes, placing waypoints, creating elevation profiles, and many other mapping functions, as well as exchanging data with GPS receivers. Browsable maps are available free online.

Moagu

Moagu (http://moagu.com/) is a program that can convert and upload USGS 1:24,000 topographic maps to selected Garmin GPS receivers.

National Geographic Topo!

Topo! (www.natgeomaps.com/topo.html) is available in state or regional coverages for the entire United States. Topo! includes high-resolution scanned USGS topo maps at scales of 1:500,000, 1:100,000, and 1:24,000. It works with most GPS receivers, and can transfer GPS data to your computer in GPX format. A variety of tools let you draw freehand trails and routes and convert them to GPS routes. You can place waypoints and create GPS routes directly and view elevation profiles. You can also attach notes and photos to your map files.

USGS

You can download USGS topo maps in PDF format for free at store.usgs.gov/. You can use a plotter or wide-carriage printer to print a map on a single sheet, or you can print each map on four sheets of letter paper.

GPS Babel

Although not a mapping program, GPS Babel (www.gpsbabel.org) is an essential tool for anyone who uses GPS data. It converts between nearly every GPS format, including proprietary formats such as Topo!'s TPO, and works with GPX data and most GPS receivers.

GPS Visualizer

GPS Visualizer (www.gpsvisualizer.com) is a Web site that lets you upload GPS data in many different formats, display it in Google Earth and Google Maps, plot the data as images and elevation profiles, and export to GPX format.

Get Set

Receivers

Basic Setup

Custom pages on a GPS receiver: Most GPS units let you customize the data that is shown on the various pages. In this book, I assume you are using the default pages, unless otherwise noted.

For use in the field, away from vehicle power, you should go to the system setup page on your GPS and ensure that it is set to "Battery Saver" or the equivalent, if available. In this mode the GPS takes fewer fixes from the satellites, which greatly extends battery life.

If you're using NiMH rechargeable batteries, set the battery type to NiMH to avoid false low-battery alerts. NiMH batteries put out less voltage than single-use batteries.

Calibrating a GPS Receiver's Magnetic Compass

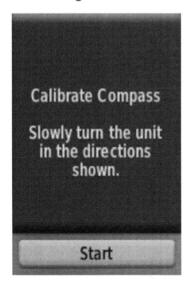

Calibrating the 3-axis magnetic compass on a Garmin trail GPS

Magnetic compasses should be calibrated after changing the batteries, or if the GPS receiver hasn't been used for some time or has been moved very far since the last use. It's a good idea to calibrate the compass just before leaving a trailhead, but make sure you are away from your vehicle and other metal objects. To calibrate the compass on a Garmin trail GPS receiver, go to the compass page, press "MENU" and select "Calibrate Compass." Select "Start" and then follow the instructions on the screen.

Digital Maps

Setting up National Geographic Topo

You'll develop your own preferences as you use Topo!, but for the examples in this book, make the following settings from the View | Preferences and Settings menu:

Units:

- Coordinates: UTM and WGS84 Datum

- Distance: Miles

- Elevation: Feet

Print/Exporting:

- Marginalia: Header and Grid Labels checked

- Notes and Photos: Include coordinates checked, all others unchecked

- Magnification: 1:24,000

Tools: Compass, set to Degrees and Decimal Minutes, True North, Full Circle, and Radial

GPS:

- Receiver Type: Set to your make and model

- Connection Type: USB for all current GPS receivers

- Waypoint Display: Set Show Waypoints, Name Only, Backdrop Off

How It Works

The Global Positioning System is the simplest and most accurate navigation system ever devised. GPS provides precise three-dimensional position (location and altitude), as well as accurate time, to users with inexpensive receivers virtually anywhere on Earth. But the hardware and software behind GPS are exceedingly complex.

NavStar Satellites

GPS navigation signals are transmitted from a constellation of 24 active satellites, backed up by several on-orbit spares. A network of ground control stations constantly monitor the satellites and adjust the orbits and the onboard clocks of the satellites. The GPS satellites and ground stations are operated by the U.S. Air Force, but anyone with a GPS receiver can freely use the system.

The satellites are placed in orbits 12,000 miles above the Earth, arranged so that at least four satellites are always visible from every point on earth. Each satellite broadcasts a microwave signal earthward that contains precise information on the location of all the satellites in the system, as well as accurate timing data. Your GPS receiver picks up these very weak radio signals and measures the time it took for the radio signal to reach the receiver. With this time information, the receiver can compute the distance to each satellite to within 10 meters (33 feet), which is quite a feat over a distance of more than 12,000 miles. Using the distance to four or more satellites, the GPS unit can calculate your position using spherical trigonometry. By calculating position fixes at intervals of a second or less, the GPS receiver can compute your speed and direction.

Errors

A number of factors degrade the accuracy of the calculated GPS position. The worst of these is atmospheric propagation. Radio signals travel through the atmosphere at slightly different speeds, depending on weather, clouds, solar activity, and the state of the ionosphere. These sources of error limit the accuracy of civilian GPS to 10 meters.

Since the NavStar GPS system was developed by and for the U.S. military, the military must have a way of denying the benefits of GPS to an enemy. One way this can be done is with "Selective Availability", or SA. With SA active, the civilian GPS signals are deliberately degraded to reduce accuracy to about 100 meters. The military has its own encrypted GPS signal from each satellite which is more accurate than the civilian signal. SA was used until May 1, 2000, when it was turned off in recognition of the growing civil uses of GPS worldwide. Also, the development of differential GPS meant than anyone could eliminate the SA-induced error. The latest generation Block III GPS satellites don't include SA capability, so it's unlikely SA will ever be used again.

Instead of relying on SA, the U.S. military has developed a battlespace jamming system to deny an enemy the use of GPS over a defined area, without having to disrupt the global system. Pilots flying over the continental U.S. sometimes are notified via official Notices to Airmen that they may lose GPS signals near military bases when testing or training is occurring. These disruptions don't usually affect ground users, except those very close to a military base.

For additional technical information on GPS, see www.gps.gov.

Into the Future

Future GPS satellites will provide additional civilian signals which will increase the accuracy of the system and also provide system integrity monitoring so that critical users, such as aircraft on precision approaches to a runway in poor visibility, will receive immediate warning of system failure or degraded accuracy.

Clearly, GPS and digital mapping will evolve into a world-wide collaboration, where governments, private entities, and individuals all contribute their expertise and resources toward maintaining an ever-changing, multi-layer, electronic representation of the Earth. Users will be able to pull out specific data that answers their needs, whether they are recreational or professional. Already the U.S. is starting to transform the airspace over the continent from one where airliners follow invisible electronic airways between ground-based radio navigation stations and are tracked by elaborate and expensive radar stations, to one where each aircraft reports its GPS position and speed directly to air traffic controllers and all nearby aircraft, so that everyone can fly directly to their destination and also receive in-cockpit warnings of potential conflicts. This is a first step toward a system that will optimize each flight path for weather and distant traffic.

GPS Everywhere

GPS receivers are now available as standard chipsets and are already ubiquitous in products such as cellular telephones, where GPS now ensures that emergency dispatchers can locate a caller. Eventually, GPS receivers will be attached to anything that needs to be tracked and safeguarded. These will include boxes in a parcel delivery system and small children on camping trips. Robotic aircraft and machines will be able to operate in places too hazardous for humans, and do so with unerring precision.

Interactive Maps

The cartographer's art will never be obsolete, but in the digital, networked world, maps are becoming a base for the world community to not only inscribe their experiences, but also become map-makers themselves. It is already impossible for government cartographers to keep maps of an entire country up to date. In the near future, governments will create the base maps and images from national resources such as earth-observing satellites, and recreational users as well as professionals will continuously review and update the details.

Total Picture

A popular science fiction novel describes a wilderness guide using a GPS-based wrist display that not only tracks her group's position on a real-time moving map, but also overlays that map with real-time weather as well as satellite imagery so detailed she can pick her way around obstacles in the terrain that she can't see from the ground.

Pilots of small general aviation aircraft are already using such capabilities. They have panel-mounted and hand held GPS receivers that provide not only near real-time weather but also terrain mapping so detailed that the receiver shows high terrain and obstacles, warns of nearby aircraft, and provides synthetic vision that allows the pilot to see the runway environment on the screen even though the real world is obscured in fog. It's just a matter of time before such detailed information is available to outdoor users on the ground, as well as scientists doing field research. To achieve worldwide coverage in remote areas, such a system will have to be satellite-based.

Of course, none of these GPS and mapping-related developments will make older skills obsolete. In the science fiction story I just described, the world satellite system is suddenly sabotaged, and our intrepid guide is thrown back on her traditional mountaineering and outdoor skills. Without them, she and her party would not have survived. Most of us are not put in such extreme circumstances, but it is true that broader outdoor knowledge and skills help make your wilderness experiences easier and a lot more fun. GPS and digital mapping is one more arrow to add to your quiver of outdoor skills.

About the Author

The author was given a GPS receiver for his birthday just as the GPS system was becoming fully operational. The unit had no mapping capability but could accurately record tracks and waypoints, just like the modern units. That basic GPS receiver completely changed the way the author mapped trails for his guidebook projects, and he has never looked back.

The author has been hiking, backpacking, and cross-country skiing throughout the American West for more than 40 years. He participated in the technical first ascents of the last major summits to be climbed in the Grand Canyon, including Buddha Temple, Holy Grail Temple, the striking pinnacle at Comanche Point, Malgosa Crest, and Kwagunt Butte. Bruce has spent more than 400 days hiking in the Grand Canyon. He continues to enjoy long backpacking treks in the more remote sections of the Grand Canyon, as well as hiking and backpacking trips elsewhere in the American West.

Outdoor writing and photography have long been serious interests of Bruce's. His first published article was in a local Arizona outdoor magazine 35 years ago, and he has since been published by Backpacker Magazine and several regional publications. About 20 years ago, his writing focus expanded to include books, with the publication of Hiking Arizona with Stewart Aitchison. He has since written more than 35 published books.

Earlier, Bruce worked eleven seasons as a wildland fire fighter for the U.S. Forest Service and Bureau of Land Management. His positions included fire lookout, engine foreman, helitack foreman, fire station manager, and incident commander.

He was part owner of an outdoor shop for eight years, selling hiking, backpacking, climbing, and skiing gear. He started and continues to run a successful computer consulting business, offering personal computer support and Web site design to individual clients and small businesses.

Bruce has been a professional pilot for more than twenty years, and holds an Airline Transport Pilot certificate with multiengine rating. He also holds a Flight Instructor certificate with instrument rating. Currently, he is an active, part-time air charter pilot with 8,000 hours flight time.

Also by the Author

Grand Canyon Guide: Your Complete Guide to the Grand Canyon

Exploring Great Basin National Park: Including Mount Moriah Wilderness

Complete 2012 User's Guide to the Amazing Amazon Kindle (with Stephen Windwalker)

www.BruceGrubbs.com

bruce-grubbs.blogspot.com

TravelsWithKindle.blogspot.com

The author on a Nevada summit

Index

Made in the USA
Lexington, KY
30 November 2012